VIETNAMESE STREET FOOD

Tracey Lister and Andreas Pohl

Photography by Michael Fountoulakis

hardie grant books
MELBOURNE · LONDON

CONTENTS

CHOPSTICKS AND TOOTHPICKS

Street Food Culture in Vietnam

It is still dark when Ms Thuy sets up her stall on the unpaved roadside opposite a lane that leads to a high-rise of serviced apartments for well-to-do expatriates and locals. Not much is needed to get the stall going: a charcoal burner, a tarpaulin strung up with the help of two bamboo poles, a trestle table on which the food is laid out, and an assortment of blue plastic stools.

At early light the first customers start to drift in. People on their way to work or coming off night shift stop by for a quick bite to eat. Hunched over their bowls, they enjoy the company of fellow diners, or some quick banter with the proprietor or the bicycle repairmen next to the stall. By 10 o'clock it's all over and everything is being packed up to make way for the tea stall that has the spot for the rest of the day.

It is often said that life in Vietnam happens on the streets. This is particularly true in the overcrowded inner cities, where it sometimes seems that the Vietnamese conduct their daily life, if not exclusively on the sidewalk, then in plain view of the streets, throwing the doors to their living rooms open to the footpath. The strict division between public and private spheres is blurred when people wash their hair, clean dishes, conduct business or catch up with friends on the pavements of the cities. Eating on the street also plays an important part in daily life.

Com Bui – Dust Meals

Everywhere, something is cooking, steaming or frying in pots, pans and woks on burners fuelled by lumps of honeycomb-like coal, delivered on impossibly overloaded bicycles.

The Vietnamese version of alfresco dining is such a natural extension of street life, so widespread and common, that it is easy to overlook how fairly recent the phenomenon of the so-called *com bui*, literally 'dust meals', really is.

Traditionally, family meals at home were sacred, but historical upheavals and changes in work practices created an eating culture with roving food vendors and street stalls to feed the hungry masses away from their houses. The wars for national independence against the French and the Americans from 1945 to 1975 displaced scores of people, and the Doi Moi policies of economic renewal at the end of the 1980s introduced modern work practices that meant longer hours and often greater distances between home and work. These changes revolutionised not only the way the country was run, but also the way the country ate.

Still, there is more to the popularity of *com bui* than politics and economics – kerbside dining fits Vietnam's collectivist culture of doing things together. Eating alone is frowned upon, so much so that the Vietnamese have coined a saying, 'an mot minh dau tuc', which literally means 'eating alone is painful'. Luckily, squeezing in at a communal table on low stools or wobbly child-size plastic chairs, close to the street life and the traffic, is the very opposite of private dining. Even if one eats alone, one isn't lonely, but connected to fellow diners and the surrounding community.

The shift from eating at home or in more up-market restaurants to casual kerbside dining also marks a transition from a feudal, class-ridden society to a more equal one – a new society, where peasants and public servants, students and shop owners can share a bench and slurp their noodle soups side by side.

Making a Living on the Street

The huge social changes Vietnam went through in the last century were a great leveller in more ways than one. The social and economic pressures fuelled the popularity of, and necessity for, street food. By the same token, though, hard times forced many a family, as a popular Vietnamese proverb goes, 'to make one's living on the street'. Devoid of any red-light-district connotations, it refers to supplementing the household income by running a small business where all family members can pitch in: a shop out of the front room, a tea stall on the pavement, or a food stall.

The advent of street food might have been closely related to the long struggle for independence, but after the end of what the Vietnamese call the American War, street food culture faced significant difficulties. Food was in short supply and was rationed during the *bao cap* or so-called 'subsidised period', which lasted well into the 1980s. During that time, the government put tight restrictions on operating small businesses. However, food stalls carried on, flying under the radar of the authorities, often operating out of private homes or with restricted trading hours. Soon after the introduction of economic reforms in 1986, the street food scene blossomed again and the whole range of culinary delights returned to the city pavements.

For many vendors, a cherished family recipe became the springboard into the hospitality industry. And while it is mostly the women who take the plunge into opening their own businesses, family recipes are rarely passed on to the daughters. Instead it is the daughter-in-law who commonly benefits from learning the kitchen secrets. This is particularly true in the more traditional country areas. Since women usually move in with their husbands' families, who might even live in different villages or towns, withholding recipes is an effective form of 'copyright protection', ensuring the culinary knowledge stays strictly within the one family.

Com Binh Dan and One-dish Joints

The fondness for kerbside dining gave rise to new kinds of eateries.

At one end of the spectrum is the *com binh dan* (literally, 'food for the working people'), probably best described as a Vietnamese lunch buffet. At these eateries, staff heap mounds of steamed rice onto plates. Diners then select what they would like to have piled on top of the rice, usually choosing from a dozen or more trays of pre-prepared dishes. The cost of the meal depends on what and how much was ordered. Food choices range from the very simple, such as roasted, salted peanuts or the ubiquitous *xao mong* (sautéed water spinach), to more elaborate fare such as fish in caramel sauce and beef in betel leaf. It pays to arrive early, as *com binh dan* eateries often run out of the more popular dishes. Also, there are usually no bain-maries, thus an early lunch means a warm lunch.

While the *com binh dan* is all about choice, the restaurants at the other end of the spectrum offer none whatsoever. There is no lingering over trays of food, no procrastination over what to order, no discussions with the proprietor over the day's special. These eateries prepare one dish, and one dish only.

One of the most famous of these kind of eateries is Cha Ca La Vong in Hanoi, which has evolved from its humble street food beginnings at the end of the 19th century into a small restaurant and a Hanoi institution. It is so famous, it even gave its name to the street on which it is located. The only dish that has ever been served in Cha Ca La Vong's long history is pan-fried Red River fish with turmeric, dill and peanuts on cold vermicelli noodles. The current proprietor, Ms Loc, is rumoured to be the only person who knows the secret recipe for the unique turmeric marinade, which she learned from her mother-in-law in the early 1970s.

Location, Location, Location

Although food stalls can be found on virtually every street corner, location still matters. Convenience counts, as only a few places become well known enough for street food connoisseurs to go out of their way in search of the perfect *pho* or *bun cha*. The areas around markets are always street food hubs, close to vital ingredients and a steady stream of customers, hungry from hours of tough bargaining. Office areas are also popular, particularly for *com binh dan* eateries in the lanes off the main thoroughfares. Itinerant vendors set up close to their customers: sweets near schools or hearty after-work snacks near bus stops.

The street food culture is under threat from a push to gentrify and modernise neighbourhoods. Culinary reality, though, often barely keeps pace with the brave new world of bureaucratic rules and regulations. In theory, for example, meat should only be transported in refrigerated vans. In practice, hardly any of the small butcher shops can afford such a luxury. A freshly butchered pig's carcass slung over a motorbike on the way to the market continues to be a common sight, providing countless photographic opportunities for visitors and, for locals, the reassurance that the old ways of doing things might not change that quickly after all.

To combat traffic congestion and to tidy up the chaos of street stalls, parked motorbikes, and shop merchandise spilling onto the footpath, local authorities have declared some larger thoroughfares 'model streets' and are cracking down on roving street vendors. One such area is the so-called 'international *bia hoi* corner' in Hanoi's old quarter: a busy intersection with street-side watering holes selling cheap fresh beer. Rather than being driven away from their beer-drinking customers, the women selling the chargrilled dried squid elect to play cat and mouse with the police. Warned of police patrols by punters or the *bia hoi* proprietors themselves, they quickly pack up their small braziers, plastic plates and bags of dried cuttlefish and disappear into the dark lanes, only to re-emerge once the threat to their livelihood has passed. In most areas, though, the old Vietnamese proverb *'phep vua thua le lang'* ('The King's rule has to yield to the village custom') continues to apply. In practice, this means that it is the occupant of the house who determines what can and cannot happen on the pavement in front of it – like subletting a space that is, strictly speaking, public property. The custom appears to be tolerated by the authorities, and a whole range of arrangements is in place, from street sellers being simply accepted at certain times of the day, to more formal 'rental' agreements.

The push for gentrification and squabbles over the use of sidewalks drive many vendors away from the main streets into smaller alleyways. Although it might be more difficult to seek out specific stalls, a stroll through the mazes of alleys and lanes often ends up being a journey of discovery leading to more memorable meals in more picturesque surroundings than the main street would ever be able to offer.

Pho, Glorious *Pho*

Street food also satisfies another aspect of Vietnamese culinary culture: a fondness for grazing, for eating smaller dishes and snacks throughout the day instead of a couple of big meals at set times. Street stalls have very specific trading hours, and roving vendors often only set up during the best times for their specialty. While there is an extensive range of meals, snacks and treats to explore, and regional differences to discover, certain classics stand out. The most famous, undoubtedly, is *pho* (noodle soup), the quintessential Hanoi street food and, in the words of the venerable scholar, Huu Ngoc, no less than 'Vietnam's contribution to human happiness'. *Pho* is treated as a national treasure, so much so that the soup even warranted a conference some years ago, covering the social, culinary and historical aspects of the dish.

The origins of *pho* are shrouded in mystery. It seems that it was invented in the early 20th century in the province of Nam Dinh, which was then a centre of the French colonial textile industry. One theory contends that it was a blend of French (beef) and Vietnamese (noodles) influences. Another claims that the name *pho* was chosen as a phonetic imitation of the French word *feu*, as in *pot-au-feu*. From a strictly linguistic point of view, *pho* is the name of the rice noodles used in the soup, but the word stuck as shorthand for the entire dish. What seems certain is that the impoverished village of Van Cu is the epicentre from which *pho* started its victory march to street food glory. The first documented villager to move to Hanoi to earn a living as a *pho* vendor was a Mr Van in 1925. Many more were to follow in his footsteps, particularly after the end of World War II when the dish started to grow in popularity.

Pho started out as a beef soup in three basic varieties: with slices of boiled and air-dried beef (*pho bo chin*), with thin slices of rare beef (*pho bo tai*) or a mixture of both (*pho bo tai nam*). *Pho* with chicken (*pho ga*) was initially considered a soup for women and children, and before 1945 only one stall in Hanoi made *pho ga*. It only became more widespread in the years immediately after the Japanese occupation of Vietnam and then again during the *bao cap* era – both times in which beef was hard to come by. Nowadays, the soup is a well-loved alternative to the heavy *pho bo*, particularly during the oppressive heat of summer. Although *pho* is originally a northern dish, it has been adopted by the south and the recipes changed in the process. In Ho Chi Minh City, *pho* is served in bigger bowls with more herbs and other condiments, a custom considered vulgar by many of the northern *pho* purists.

Bread and Noodles

Pho might be the most famous street food, but hot on its heels in the popularity stakes is another street eats treat, *bun cha*: chargrilled pork patties floating in a tangy dipping sauce, served with cold vermicelli (*bun*) and an assortment of herbs and salad leaves. It is often served with *nem ran*, fried spring rolls, on a separate plate.

Eating *bun cha* can test the chopstick skills of the Western diner: using the implements to make a lettuce leaf parcel with vermicelli, meat and herbs to dip into broth takes some practice. If that is too fiddly, a mouthful of vermicelli and meat, followed by a lettuce or herb leaf, will also do the trick.

While *pho* is traditionally a breakfast or early dinner, *bun cha* firmly occupies the lunchtime slot, and it is the enticing aroma of the grilled pork that lures in the diners. The writer Thach Lam (1909–1942), who penned one of the first books on Vietnamese food, *Delicious Hanoi Food*, even went so far as to claim that a whiff of the delicious smell of the marinated pork being grilled would be enough to make the ill rise from their sick beds.

For a change from rice noodles, one doesn't have to look far. The French left Vietnam in 1954 after being defeated by the Viet Minh in the northern mountain town of Dien Bien Phu, but they left behind an enduring love for fresh, crusty baguettes, *banh mi*. As with most foreign food, the Vietnamese adapted the original recipe to suit their tastes. Here, baguettes are made from a wheat and rice flour mixture, which results in a very airy bread that has a thin crisp crust and looks like an oversized, oblong roll.

The bread is peddled by roving street vendors carrying bamboo baskets covered with hessian sacks to keep the baguettes warm, or from street stalls, where they are artfully arranged into pyramids.

The local version of the sandwich has a firm foothold in the local street food culture. Vietnamese–American author Monique Truong (*The Book of Salt*) has called it 'the ultimate on-the-go fare'. Only fitting, then, that *banh mi* is particularly popular in fast-paced Ho Chi Minh City, where vendors cram them full of delicious fillings, ranging from a whole array of cold meats, to omelette and fish patties, all spiced with pickles, fish sauce and chilli.

The latest addition to the *banh mi* family is a culinary nomad: the doner kebab. Originally imported to Germany by guest workers from Turkey, it was brought to Vietnam by chef Tran Minh Ngoc, who worked in Augsburg in the late 1990s. Ngoc opened his first kebab grill in 2005 in front of the German cultural institute in Hanoi and over the last few years, the doner kebab has become the fastest growing street food in the city, with carts popping up everywhere. But Vietnam wouldn't be Vietnam if it didn't put its own spin on the Middle Eastern staple: the *banh mi* is made with grilled pork instead of halal lamb and might even come with a dash of fish sauce.

Fast Food Nation

Late arrivals, like the kebab, notwithstanding, the street eats game is inherently conservative. It's about tradition, not experimentation. It is about dishes that have been perfected over years and even decades, and which are not to be tampered with.

Vietnamese street food culture remains a bastion of cultural identity against culinary globalisation. Despite the advent of food chains in Ho Chi Minh City and Hanoi, and the disappearance of the traditional wet markets, stalls on every corner continue to offer the uniquely Vietnamese version of fast food: cheap and cheerful, fresh and nutritious, seasonal and local, for a people perpetually on the move.

ABOUT THE RECIPES

Selecting a limited number of dishes for this book has been a tricky task. Vietnam's street food is as diverse as the country itself: a country that boasts highlands of a rugged beauty and a 3000-kilometre coastline, Indochina's highest mountain and two deltas, the sprawling metropolises of Hanoi and Ho Chi Minh City, and a countryside that is home to 54 ethnic groups.

First and foremost, the recipes in this book represent the food we love to eat on the street. At the same time, we tried to balance the selection by choosing dishes from across the country as well as covering a variety of different cooking methods, ranging from deep-frying to dry-steaming. No book on Vietnamese street food would be complete without classics such as *bun cha* or *pho ga*, but we also included some equally delicious, lesser-known dishes such as duck rice porridge, and tofu and green bananas with turmeric.

We have divided the recipes into seven chapters – five on savoury dishes, one on sweets and a separate section on the various dipping sauces and condiments that accompany every Vietnamese meal. The dipping sauces are generally constructed around fish sauce, vinegar or lime juice, and sugar. The ratios depend on the dish with which the sauce is being served and each recipe has a cross-reference to the correct dipping sauce.

The first chapter is dedicated to spring rolls, probably Vietnam's most well-known culinary export. Prawn and pork are the varieties most often served in Vietnamese eateries outside the country, but almost every region in Vietnam has its own distinct signature roll or wrap.

The next two chapters group recipes where the preparation requires slightly more effort, but the results are rewarding. Grilling and roasting, and boiling and steaming, are very popular with marinated meats and poultry, and the charcoal barbecue dishes make great beer food – ideal for summer grill parties in the backyard.

The chapter on stir-frying and deep-frying describes the most popular cooking methods on the streets. The ingredients come together quickly and all that is needed is one cooking station, sometimes nothing more than a wok and a piece of honeycomb charcoal in a tin can. Similarly, the final section on baguettes and salads focuses on dishes that are easy to prepare with access to limited cooking facilities.

Rice is essential in any Vietnamese meal, but cooking steamed rice can be difficult on the street. Many street food specialities use sticky rice, which is traditionally eaten for breakfast or as a late-night snack. Another alternative to steamed rice is rice noodles, which are very transportable and can be eaten cold or heated up in a broth. We have described some of the different kinds of noodles, ranging from the soft, fresh *bun* (vermicelli) to the dried, very thin *mien* (cellophane noodles), in the glossary, along with the herbs that give the Vietnamese dishes in this book their distinct aroma.

The recipes finish with sweet dishes. Traditionally, the Vietnamese don't eat desserts at the end of a meal, preferring freshly cut fruit. That is not to say that they don't have a sweet tooth, which is satisfied with snacks in between meals. In the cooler climate in the north, these often take the form of sweet soups, which make perfect winter warmers.

Street food is fast food. Once the ingredients have been set up, putting the dishes together is quite quick and easy. Unpretentious, fresh and with an emphasis on flavour over presentation, they are ideal for casual dining and summer picnics.

The recipes in this book are designed for six diners. Unlike other Vietnamese recipes that form part of a banquet, street food dishes are traditionally eaten on their own. However, the recipes can be combined to make a larger meal. For a sit-down dinner for six to eight people, we recommend selecting about six dishes from the various chapters in order to give a good cross-section of cooking methods.

ROLL

BEEF RICE PAPER ROLLS

Bò cuốn nem

The rice noodle sheets in this recipe are like uncut *pho* noodles, and are available in the refrigerated section of most Asian supermarkets. In fact, the entire dish takes its inspiration from the famous beef noodle soup, *pho bo*, and turns it into a perfect summer snack.

200 g beef fillet, thinly sliced

2 garlic cloves, chopped

oil, for frying

400 g rice noodle sheets

1 butter lettuce, torn into large pieces

1 large handful coriander leaves

1 large handful mint leaves

1 carrot, cut into thin strips

½ cucumber, seeded and cut into long strips

2 tablespoons fried shallots (see page 189)

classic dipping sauce (see page 186) to serve

....
Serves 6
....

Combine the beef and garlic and set aside for 15 minutes. Heat a wok over high heat, add some oil and stir-fry the beef until browned. Remove from the wok and set aside.

Place a rice noodle sheet on a board. Arrange some of the lettuce, herbs, beef, carrot, cucumber and fried shallots in a line at one end of the rice noodle sheet and carefully roll up to form a log shape. Continue with the remaining rice noodle sheets and filling.

Arrange the rolls on a plate and serve with the classic dipping sauce.

STEAMED RICE NOODLES FILLED WITH PORK AND MUSHROOMS

Banh cuốn

These noodles can be quite tricky to make, but you can simplify the recipe by purchasing ready-made noodle sheets from the refrigerated section of an Asian supermarket. However, mastering the art of steaming your own noodles can be very satisfying.

3 dried wood ear mushrooms

2 dried Chinese mushrooms

1 cup rice flour

½ cup tapioca flour

⅓ teaspoon salt

oil, for frying

3 red Asian shallots, finely chopped

4 garlic cloves, finely chopped

1 small carrot, finely diced

250 g pork mince

2 teaspoons fish sauce

⅓ teaspoon sugar

⅓ teaspoon freshly ground black pepper

1 tablespoon fried shallots (see page 189) to serve

classic dipping sauce (see page 186) to serve

....
Serves 6
....

Soak the mushrooms in warm water for 20 minutes. Drain the mushrooms and squeeze out any excess water. Remove the stems and thinly slice the caps.

Meanwhile, prepare the batter by combining the rice flour, tapioca flour and salt in a large bowl. Add 500 ml water and whisk to form a smooth batter. Set the batter aside while you prepare the filling.

Heat the oil in a small frying pan and cook the shallots and garlic until fragrant. Add the diced carrot and cook for 1 minute. Add the pork, fish sauce, sugar and pepper and cook until the pork has coloured. Finally, add the mushrooms and cook for 1 minute. Remove the mixture from the pan and set aside.

Lightly oil a baking tray. Fill a saucepan with water. Stretch a muslin cloth over the saucepan until it has a drum-like tension. Secure it with string. Bring the water to the boil, then spoon a ladleful of batter into the centre of the cloth. Use the smooth side of the ladle to spread the batter into a small circle using a circular motion. Cover with the saucepan lid and steam for 20 seconds. Remove the lid and carefully transfer the rice noodle to the prepared tray.

Spoon 2 tablespoons of the pork mixture onto the centre of the rice noodle. Fold in the sides, lift the end closest to you, fold it over the pork mixture and roll up. Place on a platter and repeat until all the ingredients are used.

Scatter over the fried shallots and serve with the classic dipping sauce.

TOFU AND ROASTED RICE SPRING ROLLS

Nem thinh

Thinh, roasted rice flour, is often used in Pagoda cooking when no animal products, chilli or garlic can be used. The slightly nutty flavour imparted by roasting makes vegan dishes appear more substantial and adds complexity.

100 g firm tofu

oil, for frying

60 g cellophane noodles

140 g carrot, cut into thin strips

140 g kohlrabi, cut into thin strips

pinch of sugar

⅓ teaspoon salt

¼ teaspoon freshly ground black pepper

2½ tablespoons roasted rice flour

1 small iceberg lettuce, shredded

½ handful holy basil leaves

½ handful coriander leaves

24 rice-paper wrappers

vegan dipping sauce (see page 188)
  or classic dipping sauce (see page 186)
  to serve

....
Serves 6
....

Cut the tofu into 1.5 cm slices. Pan-fry the tofu in the hot oil until golden brown. Drain well on paper towel. When the tofu is cool enough to handle, cut the slices into 1 cm strips.

Cook the noodles in boiling water for 2 minutes, then drain and refresh in cold water. Drain and set aside.

Heat a little oil in a frying pan and cook the carrot and kohlrabi until softened. Season with the sugar, salt and pepper. When the vegetables have wilted, add the tofu and remove from the heat.

Cut the noodles into short lengths. Add the noodles and roasted rice flour to the vegetables and toss to combine. Add the lettuce and herbs and toss through the mixture.

Dip a rice-paper wrapper in warm water for 1 second. Do not soak the wrapper as it will become too soft and tear when rolled. Place the wrapper on a flat surface. Wait for 20 seconds, then place a tablespoon of the tofu and noodle mixture on the bottom third of the wrapper. Bring the bottom of the wrapper up over the filling, fold in the sides and then roll up. Set aside, seam-side down, while you prepare the remaining spring rolls.

Serve with the dipping sauce.

Phủ Tây Hồ

25 Phủ Tây Hồ

ƠNG HIẾU

HƯƠNG HIẾU

N· ỐC· CÁ

ÚN ỐC· CÁ

PORK SKEWERS IN RICE PAPER

Thịt lợn xiên cuốn

These Nha Trang-style pork skewers are used to fill spring rolls, which your guests can roll for themselves at the table. Green banana, pineapple or star fruit can also be added to the pork mixture as additional fillings. Also, the pork mixture can be formed into small patties and used as a filling for crusty baguettes.

600 g pork mince

1½ tablespoons roasted rice flour

3 garlic cloves, chopped

2 red Asian shallots, chopped

1 tablespoon fish sauce

1 teaspoon annatto oil (see page 191)

½ teaspoon sugar

¼ teaspoon salt

½ teaspoon freshly ground black pepper

1 sheet tofu skin

oil, for frying

600 g rice vermicelli

2 small iceberg or other crisp green lettuces, leaves separated

1 handful Vietnamese mint leaves

60 g roasted unsalted peanuts, chopped

carrot and daikon pickle (see page 190) to serve

24 rice-paper wrappers

classic dipping sauce (see page 186) to serve

....
Serves 6
....

Combine the pork, rice flour, garlic, shallots, fish sauce, annatto oil, sugar, salt and pepper in a bowl. Mix well, cover and set aside for 30 minutes. Soak 12 bamboo skewers in water for 20 minutes.

Meanwhile, use scissors to cut the tofu skin into pieces 2–3 cm wide, then cut each piece into 5–6 long strips. Heat some oil in a wok and fry the tofu skins in batches until they are golden brown. Drain well on paper towel.

Divide the pork mixture into 12 portions. Using lightly oiled fingers, form each portion of the pork mixture into a long sausage shape around a bamboo skewer.

Soak the rice vermicelli in boiling water for 4–5 minutes. Stir to separate the noodles, then drain and refresh under cold water. Use kitchen scissors to cut the vermicelli into easy-to-manage lengths.

Assemble the lettuce, tofu skin, noodles, mint, peanuts and carrot and daikon pickle on a large platter.

Dip one rice-paper wrapper at a time in warm water for 1 second. Do not soak the wrappers as they will become too soft and tear when rolled. Place on a flat surface for 20 seconds, then remove any excess water with a clean cloth. Place the prepared wrappers on a serving platter.

Cook the pork skewers on a hot chargrill or barbecue for 2–3 minutes on each side, or until cooked through. Place the skewers on a serving platter.

Invite diners to place some lettuce, tofu skin, vermicelli, mint, peanuts, pickle and meat from half a pork skewer on a rice-paper wrapper, then to bring up the bottom of the wrapper over the filling, fold in the sides and roll up.

Serve with the dipping sauce.

SPRING ROLLS WITH CHINESE SAUSAGE, JICAMA AND OMELETTE

Nem cuốn trứng, củ đậu và sốt

Roaming street vendors peddle these spring rolls from their carts in Ho Chi Minh City. The dish is a legacy of the migration of ethnic Chinese to southern Vietnam, many of whom settled in the Cholon (literally 'big market') district. Traditionally, the Chinese use wheat-based wrappers, but the Vietnamese have adapted the recipe to suit local tastes and use rice-paper wrappers.

Lap cheong sausage is a dry Chinese pork sausage that has a slightly sweet taste with a hint of cassia. It is readily available in Asian supermarkets. Jicama hails from Central America. It made its way to the Philippines on Spanish ships and from there it reached Vietnam and its neighbours. The starchy root can absorb a variety of flavours and is mainly used for its crunchy texture, which is similar to that of water chestnuts or nashi pears.

48 dried shrimp

3 lap cheong sausages

8 eggs

oil, for frying

3 garlic cloves, chopped

24 rice-paper wrappers

1 butter lettuce, leaves separated

1 jicama, peeled and cut into thin strips

1 handful Thai basil leaves

hoisin dipping sauce (see page 187) to serve

....
Makes 24
....

Cover the dried shrimp with warm water and set aside while you prepare the remaining ingredients.

Cook the lap cheong sausages in a frying pan, turning, for 5–6 minutes, then drain well on paper towel. Cool slightly, then cut on an angle into 3 mm slices.

Break 2 eggs into a small bowl and whisk to combine. Heat a little oil in a non-stick frying pan. Pour the egg into the pan and gently stir for 5 seconds, spreading the egg over the base of the pan, then cook until set. Remove from the pan and repeat with the remaining eggs. Cool the omelettes, then cut into 5 mm strips.

Drain the shrimp, reserving the soaking liquid to make the dipping sauce. Heat a little oil in a pan and fry the garlic until fragrant. Add the drained shrimp and cook for 3–4 minutes. Set aside to cool.

Dip a rice-paper wrapper in warm water for 1 second. Do not soak the wrapper as it will become too soft and tear when rolled. Place the wrapper on a flat surface. Wait for 20 seconds, then place a lettuce leaf, some omelette strips, jicama, basil, sausage and 2 dried shrimp on the bottom third of the wrapper. Bring the bottom of the wrapper up over the filling, then fold in the sides and roll up. Set aside, seam-side down, while you prepare the remaining spring rolls.

Serve the spring rolls with the dipping sauce.

SEAFOOD SPRING ROLLS

Nem hải sản

These unusual rolls hail from the north of Vietnam, and are much heartier than the southern variety. The dish also borrows some French culinary ingredients, breadcrumbs and mayonnaise, and incorporates them into one of Vietnam's most iconic dishes – the spring roll.

2 lemongrass stems, white part only, crushed

3 cm knob of ginger, sliced

4 black peppercorns

½ teaspoon salt

400 g raw prawns

300 g squid, cut into 1 cm cubes

300 g white-fleshed fish, skin and bones removed, cut into 1 cm cubes

oil, for deep-frying

1 onion, diced

80 g mayonnaise

⅓ teaspoon sugar

24 small rice-paper wrappers

4 eggs

80 ml milk

400 g dried breadcrumbs

3 tablespoons mayonnaise, extra, to serve

....
Serves 6
....

Add the lemongrass, ginger, peppercorns and salt to a saucepan of boiling water and boil for 5 minutes. Add the prawns and simmer for 3–4 minutes. Remove the prawns with a slotted spoon and set them aside to cool.

Return the water to the boil, add the squid and cook for 50–60 seconds. Remove with a slotted spoon and set aside. Add the fish and cook for 20–30 seconds, then remove and set aside.

Heat a little oil in a frying pan and fry the onion until translucent. Drain off any excess oil. Set aside to cool.

Peel the prawns and cut them into pieces the same size as the squid and fish. Combine all of the seafood, onion, mayonnaise and sugar in a bowl.

Dip a rice-paper wrapper in warm water for 1 second. Do not soak the wrapper as it will become too soft and tear when rolled. Place the wrapper on a flat surface. Wait for 20 seconds, then place a tablespoon of the seafood mixture on the bottom third of the wrapper. Bring the bottom of the wrapper up over the filling, fold in the sides and then roll up. Set aside, seam-side down, while you prepare the remaining spring rolls.

Break the eggs into a shallow bowl and lightly whisk in the milk. Place the breadcrumbs in a shallow bowl. Roll a spring roll in the egg mixture and then roll in the breadcrumbs. Place on a tray and repeat with the remaining spring rolls.

Heat the oil in a deep frying pan or wok and deep-fry the spring rolls in batches until golden brown. Remove and drain on paper towel.

Serve the spring rolls with the extra mayonnaise.

BANH CUON STALL
Trần Thị Vân

Tran Thi Van laughingly thrusts a plastic container in our direction, urging us to look more closely. We oblige and find ourselves staring at a heap of dead, black bugs, vaguely reminiscent of dung beetles. Van exchanges the container for a small vial containing a clear liquid for us to smell. It exudes a heady, sweet perfume. 'It's the real thing! One drop off the top of a chopstick is enough,' she explains of the special seasoning that is added to the dipping broth for *banh cuon*, the stuffed rice-paper pancakes she prepares at her shop.

The liquid, called *ca cuong*, is a pheromone produced by the giant water bug (*lethocerus indicus*), which lives in the rice paddies, ponds and streams of South-East Asia. In the past, country folk would attract the bugs at night with a torch or lantern, and drain the liquid from their bodies. Once very common, the giant water bug is now relatively rare and while Van prides herself on using the real beetle juice, most of the *ca cuong* in the market is a synthetic copy that is produced in Thailand or China.

Van takes back her precious vial and returns to her steamers to fill another order. The cooking station outside the open shopfront is well set up: two steamers covered with cloth stretched tight as a drum, and a pot with the rice batter in front. On a low table, the fillings and toppings are ready in stainless steel bowls.

Years and years of making 600 to 800 *banh cuon* a day has ingrained the process in Van's body memory. She works fluently and with the utmost efficiency: ladling the batter onto the steamer, smoothing out the mixture with the base of the ladle, covering it with a lid to allow the crepe-like pancake to cook evenly, and finally lifting it with a flattened bamboo stick and carefully transferring the gossamer-thin sheets onto a greased tray. There, the filling of mushroom and pork is added, the pancake is rolled up and cut into chopstick-size pieces, then topped with deep-fried shallots and shredded prawns.

The dish is served with a broth flavoured with fish sauce for dipping and with a side of *cha que*, a cinnamon-spiced meatloaf, easily recognisable because of its orange-hued skin.

Now in her mid-fifties, Van is the third generation of her family in the *banh cuon* business. At the age of thirteen, she started helping at her mother's small shop in Thuoc Bae Street. Her mother passed away in 1973 and Van took over not long after her eighteenth birthday. 'I was the oldest of five children and had to take care of the family,' she says matter-of-factly.

The first two decades at the helm of the family business proved to be very difficult. The shop had to change address a number of times, and during the lean years between 1975 and the late 1980s, when food was rationed, rice was particularly hard to come by. Many of her customers were also so short of money that they resorted to bartering for their fix of the filled rice pancakes. However, Van's determination to continue with her trade worked out in the end.

Almost twenty years ago she moved to her present location in Hang Ga Street in Hanoi's old quarter, continuing to make her pancakes with the help of her now grown-up children. The only child not helping in Van's shop is her son, who, with her support, has set up his own shop in Le Van Huu Street, in the former French quarter.

PRAWN AND PORK LETTUCE ROLLS

Xà lách cuốn tôm thịt

A more recent addition to the street food culture, we suspect that this dish originated in restaurants before being picked up as a street food.

Char su pork, the barbecued pork with distinct crackling, can be bought in Vietnamese and Chinese restaurants. These little parcels make a perfect appetiser in the hotter months, with a nice contrast between the crispness of the lettuce and the smoky flavour of the pork.

24 spring onions, green part only

300 g rice vermicelli

24 small butter lettuce cups

1 handful coriander sprigs

350 g char su pork, cut into 24 pieces

12 cooked tiger prawns, peeled, deveined and cut in half lengthways

classic dipping sauce (see page 186) to serve

....
Makes 24
....

Blanch the spring onions in a saucepan of boiling, salted water for 30 seconds to make them more pliable. Plunge into iced water so they retain their colour. Remove the chilled spring onions from the water and drain well.

Soak the rice vermicelli in boiling water for 4–5 minutes. Stir to separate the noodles, then drain and refresh under cold water. Use kitchen scissors to cut the vermicelli into easy-to-manage lengths.

Place a lettuce cup on a flat surface. Put a little vermicelli and some coriander into the cup and fold over to enclose the filling. Place a piece of pork and half a prawn on top of the lettuce cup and secure them in place by wrapping a spring onion around the bundle. Tie the spring onion in a knot. Repeat with the remaining ingredients.

Serve the rolls with the dipping sauce.

FRIED SPRING ROLLS

Nem rán

The humble spring roll is sometimes used as a metaphor for a good marriage, a wonderful indication of the central role food plays in Vietnamese culture. Wedding speeches, particularly in the south, refer to the recipe in all kinds of symbolic ways. The elements of a good spring roll have to stick together, as do the partners in a marriage. Even the frying oil stands in as the symbol of romantic passion: if it is too hot, it will burn whatever it touches.

Jicama is a starchy root vegetable that can absorb a variety of flavours and is mainly used for its crunchy texture, which is similar to that of water chestnuts or nashi pears.

4 dried wood ear mushrooms

50 g cellophane noodles

1 small jicama

400 g pork mince

100 g crab meat

2 red Asian shallots, finely diced

1 egg

1 teaspoon freshly ground black pepper

12 large or 24 small rice-paper wrappers

oil, for deep-frying

classic dipping sauce (see page 186)
  to serve

....
Serves 6
....

Soak the mushrooms in warm water for 20 minutes. Drain the mushrooms and squeeze out any excess water. Remove the stems and thinly slice the caps.

Soak the noodles in hot water for 1 minute, then drain and refresh in cold water. Drain and cut the noodles into 4 cm lengths.

Peel and grate the jicama, then pat it dry with paper towel to remove any excess moisture.

Put the sliced mushrooms, noodles, jicama, pork, crab, shallots, egg and black pepper in a bowl and mix until well combined.

Dip a rice-paper wrapper in warm water for 1 second. Do not soak it as it will become too soft and tear when rolled. Place the wrapper on a flat surface. Wait for 20 seconds, then place 2 tablespoons of filling on the bottom third of the wrapper. Lightly squeeze the mixture to expel any air bubbles, and form the mixture into a cylinder. Bring the bottom of the wrapper up over the filling, fold in the sides and then roll up. Set aside, seam-side down, while you prepare the remaining spring rolls.

Heat the oil in a deep frying pan or wok and deep-fry the spring rolls in batches until golden and crispy.

Serve with the dipping sauce.

PRAWN AND OMELETTE SPRING ROLLS

Nem cuốn tôm trứng

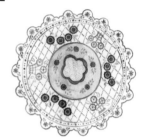

These spring rolls are very popular in the southern, tropical regions of Vietnam. Use a young pineapple rather than a ripe one, because the slight tartness of the unripe pineapple is a necessary contrast to the sweetness of the prawns and the heat of the chilli.

8 eggs

oil, for frying

200 g rice vermicelli

24 rice-paper wrappers

2 small iceberg or other crisp green lettuces, thinly sliced

1 unripe pineapple, cut into 5 cm batons

1 chilli, seeded and cut into thin strips

24 cooked prawns, peeled and cut in half lengthways

½ handful coriander sprigs

classic dipping sauce (see page 186) to serve

....
Serves 6
....

Break 2 eggs into a small bowl, lightly season with salt and pepper and whisk to combine. Heat a little oil in a non-stick frying pan. Pour in the egg mixture, gently stir for 5 seconds, spreading the egg over the base of the pan, then cook until set. Remove from the pan and repeat with the remaining eggs. Cool the omelettes, then cut into 3 mm wide strips.

Soak the rice vermicelli in boiling water for 4–5 minutes. Stir to separate the noodles, then drain and refresh under cold water. Use kitchen scissors to cut the vermicelli into easy-to-manage lengths.

Dip a rice-paper wrapper in warm water for 1 second. Do not soak the wrapper as it will become too soft and tear when rolled. Place the wrapper on a flat surface. Wait for 20 seconds, then place the lettuce, noodles, pineapple, omelette, chilli, prawns and coriander in a straight line on the bottom third of the wrapper. Bring the bottom of the wrapper up over the filling, fold in the sides and then roll up. Set aside, seam-side down, while you prepare the remaining spring rolls.

Serve with the dipping sauce.

GRILL
–
ROAST

BARBECUE PORK TWO WAYS ON RICE VERMICELLI

Bún chả

Bun cha was traditionally sold by roving vendors, who carried it in baskets hanging on poles and served it on round bamboo trays. It is now offered by countless street stalls.

This is a very popular lunchtime dish in Hanoi, where stall holders start to fan their charcoal burners midmorning, not only to increase the heat of the embers, but also to entice customers with the smoky aroma of the chargrilled, marinated meat.

25 ml fish sauce

3 garlic cloves, chopped

8 red Asian shallots, finely chopped

1 tablespoon sugar

300 g pork belly

350 g pork shoulder

1 egg

10 garlic chives, sliced

600 g rice vermicelli

bun cha dipping sauce (see page 188)

150 g bean sprouts

1 butter lettuce or stem lettuce, leaves separated

1 handful coriander sprigs

1 handful perilla leaves

....
Serves 6
....

Combine the fish sauce, garlic, shallots and sugar.

Cut the pork belly into 2 cm thick slices. Cover with half of the fish sauce mixture and marinate in the refrigerator for 2 hours.

Meanwhile, roughly chop the pork shoulder and then process in a food processor until finely minced. Place the pork shoulder in a large bowl with the egg, garlic chives and remaining fish sauce mixture. Cover and marinate in the refrigerator for 2 hours.

Soak the vermicelli in boiling water for 4–5 minutes. Gently stir to separate the noodles, then drain and refresh under cold water. Use kitchen scissors to cut the vermicelli into easy-to-manage lengths.

Using damp fingers, form the pork mince into 3 cm patties. Cook the pork patties and pork belly slices on a hot barbecue or grill for 3–5 minutes, or until grill lines appear.

To serve, divide the bun cha dipping sauce among 6 small bowls. Add three pork patties and four pieces of barbecued pork to each bowl, and put the remaining pork in the centre of the table. Arrange the noodles, bean sprouts, lettuce and herbs on another platter and place within chopstick reach. Diners dip the noodles and salad into the dipping sauce before eating them with the pork.

ROAST DUCK

Vịt quay

In Vietnam the ducks are usually prepared in street rotisseries over burning charcoal, which gives them a distinct smoky flavour. This is a street food that people take home to eat with rice and steamed greens. We have also been known to make a risotto out of it. You will need to start this recipe a day ahead.

2 kg duck

2 star anise

1 cinnamon stick

1 teaspoon Sichuan peppercorns

4 cloves

½ teaspoon ground ginger

½ teaspoon fennel seeds

3 cm knob of ginger, roughly chopped

2 tablespoons fish sauce

1 tablespoon annatto oil (see page 191)

1 tablespoon honey

2 teaspoons soy sauce

6 garlic cloves, roughly chopped

1 long red chilli, halved

4 spring onions, cut into thirds

....
Serves 6
....

Preheat the oven to 160°C (Gas 2–3). Remove the neck and any giblets from the duck and cut off any excess fat. Wash the duck under cold running water, then pat dry. Using your hand, carefully separate the duck skin from the flesh, taking care not to tear the skin.

Put the star anise, cinnamon stick, Sichuan peppercorns, cloves, ground ginger and fennel seeds on a baking tray and roast for 5 minutes, or until fragrant. Transfer the spice mixture to a mortar and grind with a pestle. Stir in the chopped ginger. Rub the mixture into the duck flesh under the skin as well as inside the cavity.

Refrigerate the duck overnight, without covering it. This allows the skin of the duck to dry out, which will help it become crispy when it is roasting.

Preheat the oven to 220°C (Gas 7). Combine the fish sauce, annatto oil, honey and soy sauce in a bowl. Rub the mixture into the duck skin and inside of the cavity. Put the garlic, chilli and spring onion inside the duck and secure with a bamboo skewer.

Place the duck on its side in a baking dish and roast for 30 minutes, basting with the pan juices. Turn the duck onto the other side and roast for a further 30 minutes. Reduce the oven to 200°C (Gas 6). Turn the duck with the breast side up and roast for 20 minutes, or until the juices run clear when a skewer is inserted into the thigh. (The duck can also be cooked on a rotisserie for about 1 hour.)

BARBECUED CHICKEN WINGS

Cánh gà nướng

In Hanoi, the legendary Ly Van Phuc Street, also simply and somewhat unimaginatively known as 'Chicken Street', specialises in this dish. Rows of stalls on each side of the street keep the barbecues burning late into the night, plying hungry revellers with tasty chicken washed down with cheap beer.

12 chicken wings

4 garlic cloves, finely chopped

2 red Asian shallots, finely chopped

⅓ teaspoon five-spice powder

1 teaspoon brown sugar

½ teaspoon freshly ground black pepper

1 teaspoon annatto oil (see page 191)

1 tablespoon fish sauce

2 teaspoons soy sauce

Serves 6

Separate the chicken wings at the joint so that the chicken cooks evenly.

Prepare the marinade by combining all the remaining ingredients. Place the chicken wings on a baking tray and pour over the marinade. Refrigerate for 1 hour, turning occasionally.

Heat a charcoal grill or barbecue and cook the chicken for 3–4 minutes on each side, until the skin is crisp and char lines appear.

CHARGRILLED DRIED SQUID

Mực khô nướng

The aroma of dried squid cooking on a chargrill brazier is a clear sign that a *bia hoi* (street-side pub) isn't far away. The salty, chewy squid, accompanied by a spicy chilli sauce, makes for a more-ish beer snack. Chilli sauce is quite difficult to make and the *bia hoi* vendors purchase theirs from the local markets.

1 dried squid

1½ tablespoons chilli sauce

....

Serves 6

....

Heat a chargrill and cook the squid for about 3 minutes on each side.

Transfer the squid to a mortar and lightly pound with a pestle to remove any of the light film from the outside.

Using scissors or your fingers, shred the squid against the grain into thin strips.

Serve with the chilli sauce and a cold beer.

BARBECUED PORK RIBS

Sườn lợn nướng

This dish has always been a crowd-pleaser, and it has the added advantage of being fairly easy to prepare – great for lazy summer Sundays. It is full of robust flavours, and barbecuing the ribs releases a mouthwatering aroma.

Ask your butcher to cut the pork ribs into manageable pieces for you. You will need to start this recipe a day ahead.

1.5 kg pork ribs, chopped

2½ tablespoons soy sauce

1 tablespoon fish sauce

3 teaspoons annatto oil (see page 191)

6 garlic cloves, roughly chopped

3 cm knob of ginger, roughly chopped

4 red Asian shallots, roughly chopped

1 long red chilli, chopped

1 tablespoon brown sugar

2 teaspoons five-spice powder

½ teaspoon freshly ground black pepper

2 star anise, crushed

1 cinnamon stick, crushed

....
Serves 6
....

Place the pork ribs in a shallow tray. Combine all of the remaining ingredients in a bowl, then pour over the ribs. Cover with plastic wrap and marinate in the refrigerator for 8 hours or overnight.

Remove the ribs from the refrigerator about 30 minutes before you are ready to cook them.

Steam the ribs on a steaming rack over boiling water for 45 minutes.

Meanwhile, heat a barbecue or chargrill. Cook the ribs on the hot grill for 15 minutes, or until grill lines appear and the meat takes on a deep golden colour.

MARINATED GRILLED BEEF ON NOODLE SQUARES

Bánh hỏi thịt bò nướng

This great southern dish also works well with char su pork.
Children love it because they get to roll it themselves. The rice
noodle squares are available from most Asian supermarkets.
If they are unavailable, you can use rice vermicelli instead.

600 g rump steak

4 garlic cloves, chopped

3 red Asian shallots, chopped

½ teaspoon sugar

½ teaspoon freshly ground black pepper

1½ tablespoons fish sauce

12 fresh rice noodle squares

1 iceberg lettuce

2 handfuls coriander sprigs

½ handful perilla leaves

1 handful mint sprigs

2½ tablespoons peanut oil

4 spring onions, green part only, sliced

classic dipping sauce (see page 186)

....
Serves 6
....

Cut the beef into slices about 1 cm thick and 4–5 cm long. Combine the beef with the garlic, shallots, sugar, black pepper and fish sauce. Set aside for 30 minutes to allow the flavours to develop.

Cut the rice noodle squares in half and arrange on a platter. Separate the lettuce into cups and arrange on a separate plate with the herbs.

Heat a chargrill or barbecue and cook the meat on both sides until done to your liking. We like it medium-rare, although on the streets the meat tends to be well done.

Meanwhile, gently heat the peanut oil and spring onion in a saucepan for 1 minute, or until the spring onion has just wilted. Remove from the heat.

Place the hot beef on the noodle squares and drizzle with the spring onions and peanut oil.

Pick up a lettuce cup and place a noodle square, along with a piece of beef and some spring onion, into the cup. Add some of the coriander, perilla and mint, and roll into a fat log. Serve with the dipping sauce.

CARAMEL FISH WITH GALANGAL

Cá kho tộ

This dish is prepared using carp at roadside stops in the Mekong Delta. Along Vietnam's almost 3000-kilometre coastline, it is made with mackerel. The version below, which uses galangal and coconut milk, is typical of the southern beach town of Nha Trang.

3–4 mackerel fillets, 2–3 cm thick

3 red Asian shallots, finely diced

2½ tablespoons fish sauce

¼ teaspoon freshly ground black pepper

1½ tablespoons sugar

oil, for frying

150 ml coconut milk

3 cm knob of galangal, peeled and cut into thin strips

1 long red chilli, cut into 5 mm rings

pinch of freshly ground black pepper, extra

4 spring onions, sliced

½ handful coriander sprigs

....
Serves 6
....

Combine the mackerel with the shallots, 1 tablespoon of the fish sauce and the pepper and set aside to marinate for 20 minutes.

Meanwhile, put the sugar and 1½ tablespoons water in a heavy-based saucepan over medium heat and stir until the sugar has dissolved. Bring to the boil and then cook until the sugar is a rich golden colour. Pour in 250 ml of water, standing away from the pan. When the spluttering has stopped, stir until the caramel sauce is smooth.

Preheat the oven to 180°C (Gas 4). Heat a little oil in a frying pan and brown the mackerel on both sides. Add the caramel sauce, coconut milk, galangal, chilli and remaining fish sauce. Bring to the boil, then remove from the heat.

Transfer the fish and sauce to a clay pot or casserole dish, cover and bake for 10 minutes. Remove the lid and bake for a further 4–5 minutes.

Serve the fish in the clay pot, sprinkled with the extra pepper, spring onions and coriander.

CLAY POT PORK WITH QUAIL EGGS AND DAIKON

Thịt lợn kho trứng cút và củ cải

This is a Vietnamese classic: a typical workers' lunch at *com binh dan* eateries and a regular at family meals. If you are using your clay pot for the first time, soak it in cold water overnight or it will crack in the oven.

800 g pork belly

100 ml fish sauce

2 garlic cloves, chopped

2 red Asian shallots, chopped

⅓ teaspoon freshly ground black pepper

6 quail eggs

1 tablespoon sugar

oil, for deep-frying

100 ml coconut milk

250 g daikon, peeled and cut into cubes

....
Serves 6
....

Slice the pork into 2 cm strips. Place in a shallow tray, add 2 tablespoons of the fish sauce, the garlic, shallots and pepper and marinate for 20 minutes.

Bring a saucepan of water to the boil. Gently lower the eggs into the water and boil for 5 minutes. Remove with a slotted spoon and plunge into cold water to stop the cooking process. Cool, then peel and set aside.

Put the sugar and 1½ tablespoons water in a heavy-based saucepan over medium heat and stir until the sugar has dissolved. Bring to the boil and cook until the sugar is a rich golden colour. Pour in 250 ml water, standing away from the pan. When the spluttering has stopped, stir until the caramel sauce is smooth.

Preheat the oven to 160°C (Gas 2–3) and place a clay pot in the oven to heat up. Heat a little oil in a wok and stir-fry the pork until browned all over. Add the caramel sauce, remaining fish sauce, coconut milk, daikon and enough water to cover the meat.

Transfer the contents of the wok to the heated clay pot and bake for 40 minutes.

Heat the oil in a deep frying pan or wok and deep-fry the quail eggs until lightly golden. Add the eggs to the clay pot and cook, uncovered, for a further 15 minutes.

BOIL
-
STEAM

STICKY RICE WITH PEANUTS

Xôi lạc

This is a favourite breakfast treat for children, who love to make little rice balls and dip them into the sesame and peanut paste. You will need to start this recipe a day ahead.

3 cups glutinous rice

1 teaspoon salt

¼ teaspoon sugar

100 g raw unsalted peanuts

Peanut and sesame dry paste

4 tablespoons roasted unsalted peanuts

3 tablespoons toasted sesame seeds

pinch of sugar

½ teaspoon salt

....
Serves 6
....

Soak the rice overnight in cold water.

Drain the rice and rinse under cold running water until the water runs clear.

Sprinkle the rice with the salt and sugar and stir through the peanuts. Put the rice in a steamer lined with a muslin cloth and steam for 30 minutes.

Remove the lid from the steamer and check that the rice is cooked. It should be tender all the way through.

To prepare the peanut and sesame dry paste, pound the peanuts and sesame seeds to crumbs in a mortar. Stir through the sugar and salt.

Eat the sticky rice by making small balls of rice with your fingertips and dipping them into the peanuts and sesame seeds.

If you are not going to eat straight away, cover the rice with a damp cloth to prevent it from drying out.

XOI STALL
Đặng Thị Sáu

Dang Thi Sau is sprinkling the bottom of a well-worn wooden mould, dark and shiny with age, with sesame seeds before deftly squeezing red sticky rice into it. She then up-ends it onto a small plastic plate and pushes out a perfectly formed rice cake. It is the first day of the lunar month and business is brisk, with customers demanding a more festive presentation than the usual banana leaf and newspaper wrapping to place on their ancestors' altars.

Red sticky rice, *xoi gac*, is particularly popular for special occasions such as weddings or *Tet* celebrations. Seeds of bitter gourd, *momordica cochinchinensis*, said to contain up to twenty times more carotene than carrots, are added during the cooking process, giving the rice its distinctive colour and a slightly nutty flavour.

However, *xoi gac* is only one of eight varieties of sticky rice that 57-year-old Sau is selling out of her open shopfront on Tran Phu Street, which she shares with a tofu vendor. Flavoured with a variety of sweet and savoury toppings, ranging from dried stringy pork and peanuts to mung bean or coconut shavings, and at only 8000 dong (60 cents) a serve, it is a cheap and tasty breakfast treat.

Sau learned the tricks of the trade from her now almost 100-year-old mother-in-law, who plied her trade as an itinerant sticky rice peddler for most of her life, walking the city streets, selling from bamboo baskets. It was a hard and uncertain life and not one Sau wanted to follow. Instead, she spent the first seventeen years of her working life as a construction worker. She is particularly proud of the fact that she was part of the crew that built the Ho Chi Minh Museum.

However, while working on an army housing project near Tran Phu Street, Sau had the opportunity to secure a simple shopfront in the area and decided to take the plunge into self-employment. Over the last two decades her shop has become a neighbourhood fixture. 'Income as a sticky-rice seller is better than in construction,' she says. 'But there are more hours and more worries.'

The secret to her success, she maintains, is selecting the best-quality grains, which is a science in itself. Historically, the cultivation of glutinous or sticky rice, *gao nep*, preceded the growing of the much more common hard rice. Sau only uses the expensive *nep cai hoa vang* variety, mainly grown in the Ha Bac and Nam Ha provinces. 'It is very important that the grains have a good perfume, are plump, not too long, not too short and evenly sized,' she says.

Preparation starts in the afternoon when she soaks the next day's sticky rice in cold water, and the workday starts at 1 am, with the rice steaming through the night before the shop opens at 6 am. Her oldest son, a university student, often helps her cope with the breakfast rush, and on most days she sells out well before noon.

 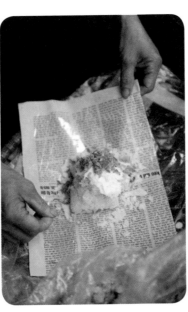 

DUCK RICE PORRIDGE

Cháo vịt

Chao is a popular winter warmer and can also be made with
fish or chicken. If you don't have time to roast your own duck,
purchase a Peking duck from your local Asian restaurant.

1 roast duck (see page 49)

6 red Asian shallots

4 cm knob of ginger

1 cup long-grain rice

oil or duck fat, for frying

1 tablespoon fish sauce

1 teaspoon sugar

½ teaspoon salt

½ teaspoon freshly ground black pepper

2 cm knob of ginger, extra, cut into
thin strips

4 spring onions, sliced

½ handful holy basil leaves, chopped

½ handful perilla leaves, chopped

4 saw tooth herb stems

ginger dipping sauce (see page 187)

....

Serves 6

....

Remove all the meat from the duck, cut into bite-sized pieces and set aside.

Use a meat cleaver to chop the duck bones into pieces. Put the bones in a saucepan and cover with cold water. Slowly bring to the boil over medium heat, removing any scum that rises to the surface. Meanwhile, put the shallots and ginger into a mortar and coarsely crush them with a pestle. Add the shallots and ginger to the stock and simmer gently for 2 hours. Strain the stock and discard the duck bones and aromatics.

Meanwhile, put the rice in a dry frying pan and cook for 2–4 minutes, or until lightly golden. Transfer to a food processor and process for 5 seconds.

Pour 1 litre of the stock into a clean saucepan and bring to the boil. In another saucepan, heat a little oil or duck fat over medium heat and fry the rice for 2–3 minutes, or until the grains start to look transparent. Pour in the boiling stock, then stir in the fish sauce, sugar, salt and black pepper. Reduce the heat and gently simmer for 20 minutes, stirring often.

Stir the duck meat and the extra ginger into the rice and simmer for 5 minutes, or until the rice is cooked. Remove from the heat and stir in the spring onion and herbs.

Spoon the rice porridge into six bowls and sprinkle with extra black pepper, if desired. Serve accompanied by the dipping sauce.

WONTON SOUP

Mí văn thắn

One thousand years of Chinese occupation, which officially ended in 938 AD, had a lasting effect on Vietnam. There is virtually no town in Vietnam without a Hai Ba Trung or a Le Thai To street, honouring the Vietnamese warriors who successfully fought against the invaders from the north. At the same time, the Vietnamese have happily incorporated Chinese culinary culture into their own, from chopsticks and rice cultivation to the wok and … wontons.

Broth

2 kg chicken bones (about 5 carcasses)

1 pig's trotter, cut into 4 pieces (ask your butcher to saw it)

½ teaspoon salt

2 dried squid

8 spring onions

½ teaspoon black peppercorns

1 teaspoon sugar

1½ tablespoons fish sauce

Wontons

5 dried Chinese mushrooms

12 raw prawns

150 g pork mince

¼ teaspoon sesame oil

pinch of sugar

¼ teaspoon salt

pinch of freshly ground black pepper

1 egg

18 wonton wrappers

500 g egg noodles

½ teaspoon sesame oil

5 bunches bok choy, leaves separated

4 spring onions, sliced

fish sauce to serve (optional)

....
Serves 6
....

To prepare the broth, wash the chicken bones under cold water and place in a large saucepan with the pig's trotter. Cover with cold water and add the salt. Slowly bring to simmering point, removing any scum that rises to the surface. Chargrill the squid over a gas burner or barbecue. Add to the broth, along with the spring onions, peppercorns, sugar and fish sauce. Simmer for 2 hours, regularly skimming the surface. Strain the broth and discard the solids.

To prepare the wontons, soak the dried mushrooms in warm water for 20 minutes. Drain, then squeeze out any excess water, remove the stems and chop the caps. Peel, devein and roughly chop the prawns. Place the prawns in a bowl with the mushrooms, pork, sesame oil, sugar, salt, pepper and egg, and mix to combine. Put a wonton wrapper on a board and spoon a teaspoon of the filling onto the centre of the wrapper. Dampen the edges of the wrapper, then draw it over the filling and pinch the wrapper around the filling, expelling any air to prevent the dumpling from bursting when cooked. Repeat to make the remaining wontons.

Return the broth to the cleaned saucepan and return to simmering point.

Bring a saucepan of salted water to the boil. Drop in the wontons and simmer for 3–4 minutes, or until cooked through. Remove with a slotted spoon and keep warm.

Add the egg noodles to the boiling water and simmer for 1–2 minutes, or until tender. Drain well. Toss the sesame oil through the noodles. Divide the noodles among six bowls and put three wontons in each bowl.

Blanch the bok choy in the broth for 1 minute. Remove and place on the noodles, along with the spring onions. Ladle the hot broth into the bowls and serve with the fish sauce, if desired.

FISH NOODLE SOUP
Bánh đa cá

Banh da noodles are a chewy noodle said to have originated
from the northern port of Hai Phong. They contrast well
with soft-fleshed fish and are used in *lau* (steamboats).
Rice noodles can be used as a substitute.

2 x 500–600 g whole fish

3 black peppercorns

2 eggs

1 tablespoon milk

1 cup plain flour

200 g dried breadcrumbs

oil, for shallow-frying

2 tomatoes, roughly chopped

2 lemongrass stems, white part only,
finely chopped

1 long red chilli

1 tablespoon sugar

3 tablespoons tamarind water (see
page 191)

600 g *banh da* noodles

4 spring onions, cut into thin strips

½ handful dill fronds

1 tomato, extra, cut into 6 wedges

1 tablespoon fish sauce

....
Serves 6
....

Remove the fillets from the fish (or ask your fishmonger
to do it for you). Set the fillets aside.

Remove and discard the gills from the fish heads. Wash
the fish heads and bones under cold water. Put the fish
heads, bones, black peppercorns and 2 litres of water in
a saucepan. Slowly bring to simmering point, removing
any scum that rises to the surface, and gently simmer
for 20 minutes. Do not boil or the stock will be cloudy.
Strain the stock and discard the fish heads and bones.

Meanwhile, cut the fish fillets into pieces about 4 cm
long. Break the eggs into a bowl and lightly whisk in the
milk. Put the flour on a plate and the breadcrumbs on
another plate. Dust the fish pieces in flour, toss them in
the egg mixture and then in the breadcrumbs, pressing
to coat the fish.

Shallow-fry the fish in the hot oil for 3–4 minutes, or
until golden brown. Drain well on paper towel.

Put the tomato, lemongrass and chilli in a mortar and
use a pestle to pound into a paste. Heat a little oil in the
cleaned saucepan, add the lemongrass mixture and stir
for 2–3 minutes, or until aromatic. Pour in the fish stock
and heat until it is simmering. Stir in the sugar and the
tamarind water.

Cook the noodles in a saucepan of boiling water for
2 minutes. Drain well, then divide among six bowls. Top
with the spring onion, dill and tomato wedges. Add the
fish sauce to the hot broth and ladle over the noodles.
Top with the crumbed fish pieces.

STICKY RICE WITH TURMERIC AND MUNG BEANS

Xôi xéo

Roaming street vendors spoon this sticky rice dish onto banana leaves as a quick morning pick-me-up. In the evening, small street restaurants serve it alongside fried chicken as part of a heartier meal. You will need to start this recipe a day ahead.

3 cups glutinous rice

200 g dried mung beans

2 cm knob of turmeric

1 teaspoon salt

⅓ teaspoon sugar

3 tablespoons fried shallots (see page 189), plus 1½ tablespoons oil reserved from cooking the shallots

....

Serves 6

....

Put the rice in a bowl, cover with cold water and leave to soak overnight. Drain the rice and rinse it under cold running water until the water runs clear.

Put the mung beans in a bowl, cover with cold water and leave to soak for 3 hours. Drain the mung beans well and place in a small saucepan with enough cold water to cover them. Bring to the boil, then reduce the heat and simmer for 30–40 minutes, until the mung beans are soft. Drain well and allow to cool slightly.

Press the mung beans between your hands to squeeze out the excess water. Form them into a large ball and allow to cool.

Peel the turmeric and pound it to a fine paste using a mortar and pestle. Sprinkle the rice with the salt and sugar, and stir through the turmeric. Place the rice in a steamer lined with muslin cloth and steam it for 30 minutes. Remove the lid from the steamer and check that the rice is cooked (it should be tender all the way through).

To serve, shave the mung bean ball over the rice. Sprinkle the fried shallots and shallot oil on top and eat the rice with your fingers.

RICE NOODLES IN PORK BROTH WITH CHICKEN, PRAWNS AND OMELETTE

Bún thang

Thang, meaning broth, is a word borrowed from the Chinese, which points to the Chinese culinary influence on this northern noodle soup. This is considered a very sophisticated, subtle dish, often prepared on special occasions such as lunar New Year (*Tet*), weddings and anniversaries. Traditionally, the qualities of a good *bun thang* have been likened to characteristics attributed to Vietnamese women: beauty, modesty and intelligence.

Cha lua is a pork paste with fish sauce, which has been steamed in banana leaf. It is available in most Asian supermarkets.

6 red Asian shallots

3 kg pork bones

1 teaspoon salt

6 dried shrimp

2 teaspoons sugar

1 tablespoon fish sauce

1 chicken breast on the bone

4 eggs

oil, for frying

600 g rice vermicelli

12 cooked prawns, peeled and deveined

200 g *cha lua* or ham, sliced

4 spring onions, sliced

1 handful coriander, roughly chopped

1½ tablespoons fried shallots (see page 189)

1 lime, cut into 6 wedges

....
Serves 6
....

Chargrill the shallots over a barbecue or gas burner for about 5 minutes, or until fragrant.

Wash the pork bones under cold water, then place in a large saucepan and cover with cold water. Add the salt and slowly bring to simmering point, removing any scum that rises to the surface. Add the shallots, dried shrimp, sugar and fish sauce to the broth and simmer for 2 hours, regularly skimming the surface. Add the chicken breast and simmer for 20 minutes. Remove the chicken and set aside until cool enough to handle. Remove the bone from the chicken and cut the meat into thin slices. Strain the broth and discard the solids. Pour into a clean saucepan and heat until simmering.

Break 2 eggs into a bowl and whisk to combine. Heat a little oil in a non-stick frying pan. Pour the egg into the pan, gently stir for 5 seconds, spreading the egg to cover the base of the pan, then cook until set. Repeat with the remaining eggs. Cut the omelettes into 5 mm wide strips.

Soak the rice vermicelli in boiling water for 4–5 minutes. Stir to separate the noodles, then drain and refresh in cold water. Use scissors to cut the vermicelli into easy-to-manage lengths.

Divide the vermicelli among six bowls and top with the chicken, omelette, prawns, *cha lua*, spring onions and coriander. Ladle the hot broth over the top and sprinkle with the fried shallots. Serve with lime wedges.

PHO GA STALL
Nguyễn Thanh Huyền

Not the shy and retiring type, Nguyen Than Huyen has a raspy voice, an easy laugh and a big heart for the customers of her popular *pho* eatery near the Chau Long market. She has been running her business, together with her husband, for the last decade.

Huyen operates out of what can best be described as a garage: a corrugated-iron roof covering the narrow gap between two buildings. Along the right-hand wall is a coal-fired cooktop for her large stockpot and a smaller one to boil water. Facing the street, a cart serves as the preparation area. Most of the bench space is taken up with bowls of lean chicken, *pho* noodles, red Asian shallots and limes. Behind the cooking station is a straight row of laminated tables, each set up with a neat tray containing chilli sauce, napkins, cutlery and chopsticks.

Huyen has been making chicken noodle soup, *pho ga*, since she joined her mother's business at the age of fifteen. Unemployed in the aftermath of the American War, her mother, Doan, decided to open up a soup stall. As with most good street food operations, the foundation of the business was a secret family recipe.

Setting up a food stall thirty years ago, in the days of food shortages and ration cards, was a gamble. However, Doan was a shrewd businesswoman, and located her stall in Lo Duc Street close to the now-defunct Nguyen Cao market. Not only were the ingredients easier to come by, market sellers and shoppers served as a ready-made customer base. Selling the soup at only 700 dong a bowl, the shop quickly became a success, even during those lean times. While prices have risen over the last three decades to a comparatively princely sum of 30,000 dong (one dollar and 80 cents), customers continue to flock to Huyen's stall to savour the taste of the Nguyen family's *pho ga*.

Although the youngest of three children, Huyen was the first to take up her mother's trade. Not only is Huyen running her own *pho* stall, but, like her mother, she has located her soup stall close to a market. Her older sister and brother have since followed suit, opening their own *pho* outlets.

The days of a soup stall proprietor are long. Huyen fires up the cooking station well before dawn. She has prepared the stock the previous afternoon so that it can sit overnight and its full flavour can unfold. Now it needs to simmer for another two hours before the breakfast crowd arrives. Most of the 250–300 bowls Huyen sells every day are eaten before midmorning. When the stall closes in the afternoon, she prepares the stock for the next day.

Asked about the secrets of a good *pho ga*, Huyen is understandably coy. She doesn't want to reveal too many details of her recipe, but says that the broth must simmer for at least five hours, and that it needs to be constantly checked: the heat needs to be adjusted, scum rising to the surface needs to be skimmed off immediately, and the seasoning needs to be fine tuned. At *Pho Huyen*, all that hard work pays off for the happy patrons who enjoy a clean, flavoursome broth – not too watery, not too strong, not too fatty and not too lean – with soft noodles, topped with moist and tender chicken pieces.

NOODLE SOUP WITH CHICKEN

Phở gà

Pho ga was invented during the Japanese occupation in the 1940s when beef was very hard to come by, which might explain why this dish is sometimes considered the poor cousin of the more famous and glamorous beef noodle soup, *pho bo*.

We like it as a lighter, more summery variation of *pho*, and it has the added advantage of taking less time to prepare in a home kitchen.

8 red Asian shallots

4 cm knob of ginger, cut in half

1.6 kg chicken

1 teaspoon salt

1 cinnamon stick

4 star anise

1 tablespoon sugar

1 tablespoon fish sauce

600 g *pho* noodles

3 spring onions, sliced

3 spring onions, extra, cut into strips

½ white onion, thinly sliced

1 handful coriander leaves

4 Kaffir lime leaves, cut into thin strips

1 lime, cut into wedges

1 long red chilli, sliced

fish sauce to serve

....
Serves 6
....

Chargrill the shallots and ginger over a barbecue or gas burner for about 5 minutes, or until fragrant.

Wash the chicken under cold running water. Place it in a large saucepan, cover with cold water and add the salt. Slowly bring to the boil, removing any scum that rises to the surface. Immediately reduce the heat, then add the shallots, ginger, cinnamon stick and star anise to the pan and gently simmer for 1 hour, regularly skimming the surface. To ensure a clear broth and moist, tender meat, do not boil the chicken.

Remove the chicken from the broth. The juices should run clear when a skewer is inserted into the thigh. Set aside to rest while you prepare the broth.

Strain the broth through a fine sieve and discard the aromatics. Return the broth to the saucepan and add the sugar and fish sauce. Gently simmer over low heat while you prepare the chicken and noodles.

Cut the breasts and legs from the chicken. Remove all the meat from the bones and slice it into strips.

Bring a large saucepan of water to the boil and cook the noodles for about 20 seconds, stirring with chopsticks to separate them. Drain the noodles and then divide them among six deep bowls.

Place the chicken on top of the noodles and then add the spring onions, white onion, coriander and lime leaf. Ladle in the hot broth. Serve with the lime, chilli and fish sauce for diners to adjust the flavour.

BRAWN

Thịt đông

Brawn is sold alongside pâté at local wet markets. It is particularly popular during *Tet*, when families like to prepare food in advance to avoid cooking during the first two days of the New Year celebrations.

2 tablespoons sugar

1 pig's ear

1 pig's tongue

1 pig's cheek

1½ tablespoons fish sauce

2 star anise

6 dried wood ear mushrooms

oil, for frying

1 teaspoon white peppercorns, crushed

fish sauce, extra, to serve

....
Serves 6
....

Sprinkle the sugar over the base of a dry saucepan. Cook over medium heat until the sugar starts to colour, then rotate the pan so that the sugar colours evenly. When the sugar is dark golden, add 2 tablespoons water, standing away from the pan to avoid being splattered by the hot caramel. Remove from the heat and set aside to cool.

Put the pig's ear, tongue and cheek in a bowl. Combine the caramel sauce with 1 tablespoon of the fish sauce and the star anise. Pour over the meat and marinate for 30 minutes.

Put the marinated meat in a large saucepan, cover with cold water and weigh down with a plate to submerge the meat. Bring to the boil, then reduce the heat and simmer for 1 hour. Cool slightly, then remove the meat. Strain the stock into a clean saucepan. Reduce over medium heat while you prepare the meat.

Meanwhile, soak the dried mushrooms in warm water for 20 minutes. Drain the mushrooms and squeeze out any excess water. Remove the stems and cut the caps into thin strips.

Peel the thick skin from the pig's tongue. Remove any fat and gristle from the meat and cut into 3 cm thick pieces. Heat the oil in a frying pan, add the meat and cook for 3–4 minutes, tossing occasionally. Add the mushrooms and white pepper and toss to combine. Pour in enough of the stock to cover the meat, then cook until the stock is reduced and sticky.

Stir in the remaining fish sauce and transfer the meat and stock to a shallow bowl. Refrigerate until the brawn has set to a jelly-like consistency. Slice and serve the chilled brawn with fish sauce.

STICKY RICE STEAMED IN LOTUS LEAF

Xôi gói lá sen

Green rice is an early autumn delicacy said to have originated half a century ago in Vong village, close to Hanoi. The village experienced severe flooding and the villagers were forced to harvest their rice early. The hungry farmers decided to make the most of the situation and roasted the grains, then pounded them using a mortar and pestle to remove the husks. They accidentally stumbled on a delicious treat that can be used to enhance dishes, or as a special snack in its own right. You will need to start this recipe a day ahead.

300 g glutinous rice

½ teaspoon salt

5 dried Chinese mushrooms

70 g lotus seeds

4 pandan leaves

1½ tablespoons chicken fat or oil

3 red Asian shallots, diced

2 lap cheong sausages, diced

2 teaspoons fish sauce

½ teaspoon freshly ground
  black pepper

2 large dried lotus leaves

3 tablespoons green rice

2 tablespoons grated coconut

60 g fried shallots (see page 189)

½ teaspoon salt, extra

3 teaspoons fish sauce, extra

....
Serves 6
....

Soak the glutinous rice in cold water for 8 hours or overnight. Drain the rice and rinse it under cold running water until the water runs clear. Sprinkle the rice with the salt, place it in a steamer lined with muslin cloth and steam for 30 minutes.

Meanwhile, soak the dried mushrooms in warm water for 20 minutes. Drain and squeeze out any excess water. Remove the stems and chop the caps.

Cook the lotus seeds in boiling water for 20 minutes, then drain.

Break the pandan leaves into small pieces, place in a mortar and pound with a pestle. Wearing a kitchen glove, squeeze the leaves to extract the juice. Discard the leaves.

Heat the chicken fat or oil in a frying pan and fry the shallots until soft. Add the diced sausage and cook for 1 minute. Add the lotus seeds, mushrooms, fish sauce and pepper and cook for a further 2 minutes. Remove from the heat.

Soak the dried lotus leaves in warm water for 3 minutes, or until softened.

Put the steamed rice in a large bowl. Add the lotus seed mixture and pandan juice, along with the remaining ingredients. Divide the rice into two portions. Lay a lotus leaf, vein-side down, in a deep bowl. Place one portion of the rice in the centre of the leaf and lightly press down. Fold the sides of the lotus leaf over the rice and place a saucer on top. Turn the lotus leaf parcel over so the parcel is sitting on the saucer. Remove the bowl. The weight of the rice will help keep the leaf in place. Repeat with the remaining lotus leaf and rice.

Place the parcels on a steaming rack over rapidly boiling water, cover and steam for 30 minutes. Remove from the heat and carefully cut the parcels open.

MOCK CRAB SOUP

Canh cua chay

On the first day of the lunar month, many Vietnamese keep to the Buddhist tradition of following a vegetarian diet to gain merit. Many classic Vietnamese dishes are prepared by using tofu or taro as a meat or fish substitute, and often they are formed to closely resemble the meat they are replacing.

150 g tofu

oil, for deep-frying

4 red Asian shallots, sliced

2 tomatoes, peeled, seeded and chopped

⅓ teaspoon sugar

½ teaspoon salt

1 litre soy milk

3 tablespoons *dam bong* or rice vinegar

300 g rice vermicelli

4 saw tooth herb leaves, cut into strips

5 spring onions, sliced

....
Serves 6
....

Cut the tofu into 3 cm cubes. Heat the oil in a deep frying pan or wok and deep-fry the tofu until crisp and golden.

Fry the shallots in another 100 ml of oil until golden. Remove the shallots with a slotted spoon and drain well on paper towel. Set the oil aside.

Heat a little oil in a saucepan. Add the tomato, sugar and salt and cook for 1 minute, or until the tomato has softened. Pour in the soy milk and slowly bring to the boil. Reduce the heat until simmering. Stir in the *dam bong* or rice vinegar. When the soup begins to appear curdled, simmer for a further 1 minute.

Meanwhile, soak the rice vermicelli in boiling water for 4–5 minutes. Gently stir to separate the noodles, then drain and refresh under cold water. Use kitchen scissors to cut the noodles into easy-to-manage lengths.

Divide the noodles and herbs among six bowls and ladle over the soup. Top the soup with the fried tofu, spring onion and fried shallots and drizzle with the shallot oil.

BRAISED BEEF WITH LEMONGRASS AND STAR ANISE

Bò Kho

Despite being a hearty stew, *bo kho* is a surprisingly popular breakfast in the tropical south and particularly in Ho Chi Minh City, where it is served with crusty baguettes. It also works well as an evening meal, served with noodles or rice.

1 kg beef topside, cubed

1 tablespoon annatto oil (see page 191)

2 lemongrass stems, white part only, roughly chopped

1 long red chilli, seeded and chopped

3 cm knob of ginger, chopped

5 red Asian shallots, chopped

4 garlic cloves, chopped

oil, for frying

4 star anise

1 teaspoon five-spice powder

⅓ teaspoon ground cinnamon

5 tomatoes, peeled, seeded and chopped

1½ tablespoons fish sauce

1 tablespoon sugar

½ teaspoon salt

2 large carrots, cut into chunks

3 potatoes, cut into chunks

....
Serves 6
....

Toss the beef with the annatto oil and set aside.

Place the lemongrass, chilli, ginger, shallots and garlic in a mortar and pound to a paste with a pestle. Heat a little oil in a saucepan over medium heat and fry the paste for 2–3 minutes, or until aromatic.

Add the beef to the pan and cook for 8–10 minutes, until browned all over. Stir in the star anise, five-spice powder and cinnamon. Add the tomato, fish sauce, sugar, salt and 1 litre of water.

Simmer for 1½ hours, or until the beef is tender. Add the carrot and potato and simmer for a further 20 minutes. Serve with crusty baguettes.

BITTER GOURD FILLED WITH TOFU

Đậu phụ nhồi mướp đắng

Steaming rids the gourd of some of the bitterness. A tasty variation is to deep-fry the gourds after steaming, which adds another dimension of flavour and texture.

6 dried Chinese mushrooms

3 dried wood ear mushrooms

2 bitter gourds

180 g firm tofu

½ teaspoon salt

¼ teaspoon freshly ground black pepper

⅓ teaspoon sugar

vegan dipping sauce (see page 188) to serve

....
Serves 6
....

Soak the mushrooms in warm water for 20 minutes. Drain and squeeze out any excess water. Remove the stems and cut the caps into thin strips.

Meanwhile, cut the gourds into 3 cm rounds. Using a teaspoon, hollow out the slices of gourd and discard the seeds.

Put the mushrooms, tofu, salt, pepper and sugar in a bowl. Mix until the tofu is smooth and creamy. Spoon the mixture into the gourd slices, then steam the filled slices of gourd for 15 minutes, or until they are tender when pierced with a skewer.

Serve the steamed gourd with the dipping sauce.

DUCK AND BAMBOO NOODLE SOUP

Bún vịt xáo măng

Preparing dried bamboo is a labour of love. It requires overnight soaking and boiling the following day, and the water needs to be changed at least once during the cooking process. It is usually only prepared at home on important occasions, such as *Tet* (Vietnamese New Year), ancestor days, or to farewell the kitchen god, Ong Tao.

Both fresh and dry bamboo have a musty, earthy flavour and perfume. The fresh variety adds crunch to this dish, and the dry one adds a chewy texture.

60 g dried bamboo

2 chicken carcasses

2 kg duck

4 cm knob of ginger, cut in half

6 spring onions

2 lemongrass stems, white part only, crushed

1 teaspoon salt

1 teaspoon sugar

1½ tablespoons fish sauce

3 cm knob of ginger, extra, cut into thin strips

120 g vacuum-sealed fresh bamboo

600 g rice vermicelli

1 handful Thai basil leaves

1 handful mint sprigs

4 spring onions, extra, cut into thin strips

3 tablespoons fried shallots (see page 189)

ginger dipping sauce (see page 187) to serve (optional)

....
Serves 6
....

Soak the dried bamboo in cold water overnight. Drain the bamboo, put it in a saucepan and cover with cold water. Boil for 1 hour, topping up the water as needed. Drain, then repeat the boiling process. The bamboo should now be tender, but still a little chewy. Drain and cool, then cut the bamboo into pieces 4 cm long.

Meanwhile, put the chicken carcasses and duck in a large saucepan and cover with cold water. Slowly bring to the boil, removing any scum that rises to the surface. Add the ginger, spring onions, lemongrass, salt and sugar. Reduce the heat and simmer for 1 hour. Remove the duck and simmer the broth for a further hour. Use a cleaver to cut the duck into bite-sized pieces. Strain the broth through a fine sieve and discard the chicken bones and aromatics. Pour the broth into a clean pan. Bring to the boil, then add the fish sauce and extra ginger.

Meanwhile, put the fresh bamboo in a saucepan and cover with cold water. Bring to the boil, then reduce the heat and simmer for 15 minutes. Drain and cool, then cut the bamboo into thin slices.

Soak the rice vermicelli in boiling water for 4–5 minutes. Stir to separate the noodles, then drain and refresh under cold water. Use scissors to cut the vermicelli into easy-to-manage lengths, then divide it among six deep bowls.

Put the fresh and dried bamboo, basil, mint, spring onion strips and duck pieces on the noodles. Ladle the hot broth into the bowls and sprinkle with the fried shallots. Drizzle with the ginger dipping sauce, if using.

FRY

WEST LAKE PRAWN CAKES

Bánh tôm Hồ Tây

In the late afternoons, families and couples flock to the banks of the famous West Lake (Tay Ho), in Hanoi, to enjoy this snack. The vendors compete by creating extravagant pyramids of prawn cakes to entice the hungry customers.

½ cup plain flour

1 tablespoon rice flour

½ teaspoon baking powder

⅓ teaspoon ground turmeric

⅓ teaspoon salt

pinch of sugar

1 egg yolk

1 teaspoon rice vinegar

10 small raw prawns

2 teaspoons fish sauce

¼ teaspoon freshly ground black pepper

100 g white sweet potato

oil, for deep-frying

vegetable pickle (see page 190) to serve

....
Serves 6
....

Sift the plain flour and rice flour into a bowl. Add the baking powder, turmeric, salt and sugar and make a well in the centre. Put the egg yolk, rice vinegar and 250 ml of water into the well and mix to form a paste. Cover the bowl with a wet cloth and set aside for 15 minutes.

Meanwhile, cut off the prawn heads. Leave the shells on and cut the prawns in half lengthways, removing the dark veins. Marinate the prawns in the fish sauce and pepper for 15 minutes.

Peel the sweet potato and cut it into 4 cm strips.

Heat the oil in a wok or a large deep saucepan. Put a metal ladle in the oil to heat up. Spoon 1 tablespoon of the batter into the ladle, add some sweet potato and two prawns and lower it into the oil. When the prawn cake floats, remove it from the ladle and cook until golden brown. Remove the prawn cake with a slotted spoon, drain on paper towel and keep warm while you cook the remaining prawn cakes.

Serve the prawn cakes hot with the vegetable pickle.

FRIED RICE CAKES WITH EGG

Bột chiên

These fried rice cakes are very common among the Chinese–Vietnamese community in Ho Chi Minh City. They can be found on the streets of Chinatown in District 5, Cholon, in the mornings. In Chinese restaurants, lap cheong sausage and daikon radish are added to the rice cake batter.

Rice cakes

½ cup rice flour

2 tablespoons tapioca flour

½ teaspoon sugar

½ teaspoon salt

6 eggs

⅓ teaspoon salt

⅓ teaspoon freshly ground black pepper

oil, for frying

soy chilli dipping sauce (see page 186)

4 spring onions, thinly sliced

1 long red chilli, thinly sliced

Serves 6

To make the rice cakes, combine the rice flour, tapioca flour, sugar and salt in a bowl. Add 300 ml of water and mix to form a batter. Set aside for 15 minutes.

Lightly oil a tray or cake tin that will fit in the top half of a steamer. Pour the batter into the tray. Place the tray in the top half of the steamer and steam over boiling water for 20–25 minutes, until a skewer inserted into the centre of the rice cake comes out clean. Remove the tray from the steamer and set aside to cool slightly.

Remove the rice cake from the tray and set aside until it is completely cold. (The rice cake can be refrigerated overnight.) Cut the rice cake into 5 cm x 2 cm pieces.

Break the eggs into a bowl, add the salt and pepper and lightly whisk to combine.

Heat some oil in a large frying pan. Fry the rice cakes for 2 minutes each side, or until golden brown. Drizzle the rice cakes with ½ teaspoon of the dipping sauce, then pour the egg mixture over the rice cakes. Use a wooden spoon or chopsticks to gently stir the egg so that the raw egg runs underneath the cooked egg. Cook for 1 minute, or until the egg is cooked. Sprinkle the spring onion and chilli over the rice cakes and remove from the pan.

Serve the rice cakes on individual plates or on a large platter, accompanied by the remaining dipping sauce.

SALT-AND-PEPPER SQUID

Mực muối tiêu

This classic is a favourite all along Vietnam's coastline. The only regional variations concern the amount of chillies: diners in the south prefer their squid with a little more heat than in the north.

Instead of frying, you can rub the chilli mix straight onto the raw squid and chargrill it on a barbecue.

4 squid

1 long red chilli, roughly chopped

3 garlic cloves, roughly chopped

2 red Asian shallots, roughly chopped

½ cup rice flour or cornflour

¼ teaspoon salt

⅓ teaspoon freshly ground black pepper

oil, for frying

lime, salt and chilli (see page 189) to serve

....
Serves 6
....

Clean the squid by holding the body with one hand and the head with the other. Gently pull, taking care not to burst the ink sac, and the head and tentacles will come away. Remove the cartilage and rinse the squid inside and out, then pat dry. Cut off and discard the head. Cut the body open and pull away the outside membrane. Rinse again and pat dry. Lay the squid on a board with the inside of the squid facing up. Score the flesh in a crisscross pattern, then cut the body and tentacles into bite-sized pieces.

Place the chilli, garlic and shallots in a mortar and use a pestle to grind to a fine paste. Set aside until needed.

Season the flour with the salt and pepper. Ensure the squid pieces are dry, then dust in the flour and shake off the excess.

Heat a little oil in a wok. Fry the squid for 1–2 minutes, or until the squid is light golden and cooked through. Drain well on paper towel.

Discard the oil and reheat the wok. Fry the chilli paste until fragrant, then add the squid pieces and toss until evenly coated.

Serve the squid with the lime, salt and chilli.

CLAMS WITH RICE CRACKERS

Hến xào xúc bánh đa

Shelled, frozen baby clams, available in most Asian supermarkets, work very well with this dish. The more exotic razor clams make an excellent alternative.

In Vietnam, large rice crackers, roughly the size of a vinyl record, are sold at local markets or by roaming street vendors. Outside Vietnam they can be purchased in Asian supermarkets. Heat them in an oven or over a grill and they will puff up within seconds.

60 g cellophane noodles

oil, for frying

2 lemongrass stems, white part only, thinly sliced

1 long red chilli, thinly sliced

500 g shelled baby clams, or 1.3 kg clams in their shells (see Note)

5 spring onions, thinly sliced

½ handful mint, chopped

2 teaspoons fish sauce

⅓ teaspoon freshly ground black pepper

6 large rice crackers

....
Serves 6
....

Soak the noodles in hot water for 10 minutes, then drain and cut into 2 cm pieces.

Heat a little oil in a wok. Stir-fry the lemongrass and chilli for 1–2 minutes, until fragrant. Add the shelled clams and toss for 2–3 minutes. Add the spring onion, mint and noodles and continue tossing. Lastly, add the fish sauce and pepper. Season with salt, if necessary.

Serve the clams on a platter with the rice crackers. To eat, place a small amount of the clam mixture on a piece of rice cracker.

Note: If you are using clams in their shells, roughly chop 1 long red chilli and 1 lemongrass stem. Add to a saucepan with 375 ml of beer. Bring to the boil, then simmer for 10 minutes. Add the clams, cover and simmer for 3–5 minutes, until the clams have just opened. Cool slightly, then remove the clams from their shells. If the clams are large, cut them in half.

CRAB WONTONS WITH TOMATO SALSA

Hoành thánh chiên

A simplified version of this dish is being sold by vendors in the historic port of Hoi An in central Vietnam: there, the ingredients are stir-fried and served on top of the deep-fried wonton wrappers. However, we like the surprise package of the enclosed wontons.

4 spring onions

350 g crab meat

100 g pork mince

2 cm knob of ginger, grated

⅓ teaspoon freshly ground black pepper

½ teaspoon salt

48 wonton wrappers

5 tomatoes

½ handful coriander leaves, roughly chopped

½ long red chilli, seeded and finely chopped

⅓ teaspoon sugar

2 teaspoons fish sauce

oil, for deep-frying

....
Serves 6
....

Thinly slice the spring onions. Set aside half the green part for the salsa and discard the remaining green part. Combine the white part with the crab, pork, ginger, pepper and salt. Mix well.

Place a wonton wrapper on a board and top with a spoonful of the crab mixture. Dampen the edges of the wrapper and then place another wonton wrapper on top. Squeeze to remove any air, then press the edges together to seal. Repeat with the remaining wrappers and filling.

To make the salsa, remove the seeds from the tomatoes, then cut the tomatoes into 5 mm dice. Place in a bowl with the reserved spring onion, coriander leaves, chilli, sugar and fish sauce.

Heat the oil in a deep frying pan or wok and deep-fry the wontons in batches until cooked through. Drain well on paper towel.

Serve the wontons hot, topped with the tomato salsa.

FRIED PORK AND QUAIL EGG DUMPLINGS

Bánh bao chiên

These hearty Chinese-inspired dumplings are usually served steamed.
However, in the cold winter months they are often deep-fried. We like
to think of them as a Vietnamese version of the calzone.

Dough

1 cup plain flour

¼ teaspoon salt

1 teaspoon dry yeast

90 ml lukewarm milk

12 quail eggs

40 g cellophane noodles

200 g pork mince

2 spring onions, thinly sliced

1 teaspoon fish sauce

¼ teaspoon salt

¼ teaspoon freshly ground
   black pepper

oil, for frying

....
   Makes 12
....

To make the dough, put the flour and salt into a bowl and make a well in the centre. Whisk the yeast into the lukewarm milk. Pour into the well in the flour and make small circular motions with your fingers to incorporate the milk into the flour. Transfer the dough to a floured board and knead until it is smooth and elastic. Place the dough in a clean bowl, cover with a damp cloth and put it in a warm spot to rise.

Put the quail eggs in a saucepan and cover with cold water. Bring to the boil, then cook for 4 minutes. Drain the eggs and run them under cold water to stop the cooking process. Peel the eggs and set them aside.

Cook the cellophane noodles in a saucepan of boiling water for 2 minutes. Drain and refresh under cold water, then cut the noodles into 3 cm lengths. Put the noodles in a bowl with the pork mince, spring onion, fish sauce, salt and pepper. Mix until well combined.

Lightly knead the dough on a lightly floured board to knock out the air. Divide the dough into 12 pieces, then roll each piece into a small disc.

Divide the filling into 12 portions. Flatten one portion of the filling in your hand. Place a quail egg in the centre and mould the pork around the egg to enclose it. Place the filling in the centre of the dough and press the edges to seal. Put the dumpling on the board with the seam touching the board and form a cup with your fingers around the dough. Make circular motions with the dough to firmly seal the dough and form it into a ball.

Heat the oil in a frying pan and cook the dumplings in batches for 4–5 minutes, or until golden brown, turning so they cook evenly. Drain well on paper towel.

BANH BAO CHIEN STALL

Chu Mai Phương & Phạm Văn Huệ

One of the most valuable skills Pham Van Hue learnt in the army was to make dough. Born and bred in Hanoi, Hue spent six years as a soldier in the south of the country, from 1977 to 1983, during which time he was also briefly stationed in Ho Chi Minh City. There, in the suburb of Cholon, he befriended a Chinese man who made and sold *quay*, the deep-fried bread that normally accompanies *pho*. Hue was intrigued and left the south with the ability to make the simple dough, based on yeast, water and flour.

When Hue was finally released from the army, he went back to his native Hanoi and married his high-school sweetheart, Phuong. Life was hard for the newlyweds in the austere years after the end of the American War, as the Vietnamese call the Vietnam War. Hue worked in a laundry and Phuong in a state-owned carpet-weaving company, but their combined income barely made ends meet.

In order to supplement their salaries they decided to set up a dumpling-making business. Hue already knew how to make the dough and together they experimented until they had perfected the filling: a boiled quail egg inside a mixture of minced pork, rice vermicelli and wood ear mushrooms.

For the first few years they worked from their home, preparing dumplings for restaurants while keeping their day jobs. But in 1990, after the post-war restrictions on opening small businesses had been lifted, they quit their jobs and set up a stall near their house in Pho Duc Chinh. Phuong and Hue have been selling their dumplings from that location ever since.

It is hard to imagine a stall set-up any simpler than theirs: two rickety benches, an odd assortment of plastic stools, a wok set over a charcoal brazier for deep-frying, some mismatched plastic crockery and cutlery.

Phuong's workday starts at 7 am when she goes to the market. 'I have to go early to get the best cuts of pork,' she says. At home she minces the meat herself, cooks the eggs and prepares the green papaya dipping sauce before making lunch for the family. After lunch, the preparations continue on the street. Making about 200 dumplings a day, the husband-and-wife team observe a strict division of labour. Hue rolls out the dough he has prepared earlier. Phuong encloses the filling and briefly fries the dumplings before placing them in a big bamboo basket.

Around midafternoon customers start to appear: factory workers who have finished their shifts, and students on their way home from school. Most buy a couple of dumplings, reheated and wrapped in newspaper: a cheap and tasty takeaway snack to tide them over until dinnertime.

'When we first started here, twenty years ago, we were the only ones selling food in the street. It was very quiet,' Hue explains. 'Now there's competition from restaurants and other street food stalls.' Not that Phuong and Hue have a lot to worry about. Competitively priced at 5000 dong (25 cents) a dumpling, they usually sell out of their delicious *banh bao* by nightfall.

TOFU, MUSHROOM AND GREEN RICE CAKES

Bánh nấm đậu phụ

These rice cakes are normally small enough to pop into your mouth. The recipe also works well with larger patties that can be chargrilled after frying, making it an ideal dish for a vegan barbecue.

10 dried Chinese mushrooms

10 dried wood ear mushrooms

⅓ cup green rice

700 g firm tofu

1 teaspoon salt

1 teaspoon sugar

oil, for frying

soy chilli dipping sauce (see page 186) to serve

....

Serves 6

....

Soak the mushrooms in warm water for 20 minutes. Drain the mushrooms and squeeze out any excess water. Remove the stems and finely chop the caps.

Put the green rice in a bowl and cover with cold water. Set aside for 10 minutes, then drain.

Place the tofu, in batches, in a muslin cloth or tea towel and squeeze out as much liquid as possible. Put the tofu in a bowl. Add the mushrooms, rice, salt and sugar and mix until creamy.

Using your fingers, form the mixture into small patties. Heat a little oil in a frying pan and fry the rice cakes until golden. Drain on paper towel and serve with the soy chilli dipping sauce.

MUNG BEAN AND GALANGAL PATTIES

Bánh chay nhân đậu xanh

Crispy on the outside, creamy on the inside, these pillows can be
very more-ish. Even though they are deep-fried we like to think that
the mung beans make them a healthy snack!

400 g dried mung beans

3 cm knob of galangal, peeled and
  roughly chopped

1 teaspoon salt

75 ml beer

oil, for deep-frying

soy chilli dipping sauce (see page 186)
  to serve

....
  Serves 6
....

Soak the mung beans in a bowl of cold water for 1 hour.

Drain the mung beans, then place in a blender with the
galangal and puree until smooth. Transfer to a bowl and
stir in the salt and the beer.

Heat the oil in a deep frying pan. Slide a dessertspoon
of the mixture into the oil and cook until golden, turning
once and taking care not to break up the patty. Drain on
paper towel and repeat with the remaining mixture.

Serve with the dipping sauce.

FIVE-SPICE EEL WITH RICE CRACKERS

Lươn xào xúc bánh đa

Eel is very common in the paddies and ponds in the countryside and many eel dishes started out as peasant food before becoming city delicacies.

This is a dish best eaten with your fingers. Break off a piece of rice cracker and use it to scoop up the eel.

2 large eels, skin and bones removed

oil, for frying

4 garlic cloves, finely chopped

3 red Asian shallots, finely chopped

2 lemongrass stems, white part only, finely chopped

1 long red chilli, seeded and finely chopped

⅔ teaspoon five-spice powder

¼ teaspoon salt

¼ teaspoon freshly ground black pepper

1 teaspoon fish sauce

½ teaspoon sesame oil

40 g roasted unsalted peanuts, chopped

1 handful coriander, roughly chopped

1 long red chilli, extra, sliced (optional)

3 large rice crackers

Serves 6

Finely dice the eel and set aside.

Heat a little oil in a wok and stir-fry the garlic, shallots, lemongrass and chilli for 1–2 minutes, or until fragrant. Add the diced eel and five-spice powder and stir-fry for 2–3 minutes, until the eel is cooked through. Stir in the salt, pepper, fish sauce and sesame oil. Toss the peanuts and coriander through the eel mixture.

Serve the eel on a large platter with the extra chilli and rice crackers for scooping.

PORK AND MUSHROOM PASTRIES

Bánh gối

Small kerbside stalls pop up in Hanoi during the cold winter months, selling a variety of fried snacks. These pork and mushroom pastries are the most popular.

8 dried wood ear mushrooms

50 g cellophane noodles

300 g pork mince

3 spring onions, thinly sliced

2 teaspoons fish sauce

¼ teaspoon salt

pinch of freshly ground black pepper

24 wonton wrappers

oil, for deep-frying

classic dipping sauce (see page 186)
   to serve

....
   Serves 6
....

Soak the mushrooms in warm water for 20 minutes. Drain the mushrooms and squeeze out any excess water. Remove the stems and roughly chop the caps.

Meanwhile, cook the noodles in boiling water for 2 minutes, then drain and refresh in cold water. Drain and set aside.

Combine the mushrooms, noodles, pork, spring onions, fish sauce, salt and pepper in a bowl.

Place a wonton wrapper on a board. Spoon 1 tablespoon of the pork mixture onto the bottom third of the wonton wrapper. Dampen the edges of the wrapper, fold down the top half to enclose the filling and pinch the edges together to seal. Repeat with the remaining wrappers and filling.

Heat the oil in a deep frying pan or wok and deep-fry the pastries in batches until golden. Drain on paper towel.

Serve hot as a snack with the classic dipping sauce.

TOFU AND GREEN BANANAS WITH TURMERIC

Đậu phụ nấu chuối xanh

The green bananas provide a starchy, almost potato-like quality to this dish. *Dam bong*, the liquid from fermented rice, contributes a certain tartness, adding one of the five essential flavours (sweet, sour, bitter, salty and spicy) that the Vietnamese believe should be present in every balanced meal. Street vendors often have big bowls of vinegar or tamarind as additional souring agents at the ready for self service.

4 green bananas

juice of ½ lemon

400 g firm tofu

oil, for frying

3 cm knob of turmeric

1 teaspoon salt

1 tablespoon oil

2 tomatoes, seeded and chopped

1 tablespoon sugar

1 tablespoon *dam bong* or tamarind pulp

6 betel leaves, cut into thin strips

1 handful perilla leaves, cut into thin strips

Serves 6

Peel off the outer layer of banana skin, leaving a thin layer of skin for texture. Add the lemon juice to a bowl of water. Cut the bananas into batons and put them in the water. This will remove some of the sticky liquid from the bananas.

Meanwhile, cut the tofu into 2 cm blocks. Heat a little oil in a frying pan over high heat and fry the tofu until crisp. Drain well on paper towel.

Using a mortar and pestle, grind the turmeric into a fine paste. Add the salt and oil. Drain the bananas and marinate them in the turmeric mixture for 15 minutes.

Heat a saucepan over medium heat. Add the banana and turmeric mixture and cook for 3–4 minutes, until the bananas have coloured. Add 1 litre of water, the tomatoes and sugar. Reduce the heat and simmer for 10 minutes. Add the *dam bong* and cook for 2 minutes. Add the fried tofu, betel leaf and perilla and carefully stir to combine.

Serve as part of a banquet with rice or noodles.

RIVER PRAWNS WITH PORK BELLY

Tôm rang thịt

This dish is a popular staple at *com binh dan* stalls all over
the country. The prawns are cooked in their shell, which gives
them a crunchy texture that nicely offsets the chewy pork belly.

200 g small raw prawns

oil, for frying

100 g pork belly, sliced

2 tablespoons fish sauce

⅓ teaspoon freshly ground black pepper

1 teaspoon sugar

5 spring onions, sliced

carrot and daikon pickle (see page 190)
   to serve

....
   Serves 6
....

Rinse the prawns and remove the heads. Pat dry with
paper towel.

Heat a little oil in a frying pan. Add the sliced pork to
the hot oil and cook for 3–4 minutes, until the pork is
golden brown. Remove the pork, leaving the cooking
fat behind.

Return the pan to the heat, add the prawns and cook
until they just change colour. Return the pork to the pan
and toss to combine with the prawns. Add the fish sauce,
pepper and sugar and cook for 1 minute, keeping the pan
moving so the sugar does not burn.

Add the spring onions and toss for about 20 seconds,
or until wilted. Serve immediately with the carrot and
daikon pickle.

FROG WITH LEMONGRASS AND CHILLI

Ếch xaò sả ớt

It is often assumed that the French introduced frogs to Vietnamese cuisine, but we like to think that it was the other way around. Vietnam's millions of paddies not only produce the country's staple, rice, but have always been a rich source of protein, providing eels, crabs, snails and frogs.

If fresh frogs' legs are not available, frozen frogs' legs can be purchased from Asian fishmongers.

2 red Asian shallots, peeled

3 garlic cloves, peeled

2 cm knob of ginger

½ teaspoon ground turmeric

6 frogs' legs

2 teaspoons plain flour

oil, for deep-frying

½ brown onion, cut into 1 cm wedges

1 carrot, cut into batons

2 lemongrass stems, white part only, sliced

2 long red chillies, sliced

2 garlic cloves, extra, sliced

1 tablespoon oyster sauce

2 teaspoons fish sauce

5 spring onions, cut into batons

1 handful coriander sprigs

....
Serves 6
....

Put the shallots, garlic and ginger in a mortar and pound into a paste with a pestle. Stir in the turmeric. Rub the paste into the frogs' legs and marinate for 20 minutes.

Dust the frogs' legs in the flour. Heat the oil in a deep frying pan or wok and deep-fry the frogs' legs in batches until crispy on the outside. Set aside.

Heat a little more oil in a wok. Stir-fry the onion and carrot for 3–5 minutes, until cooked but still crunchy. Add the lemongrass, chilli and extra garlic and cook until fragrant.

Add the fried frogs' legs, oyster sauce and fish sauce to the wok and toss to coat. Finally, add the spring onion and cook until just wilted.

Arrange the frogs' legs on a serving platter and sprinkle with the coriander sprigs.

STIR-FRIED LEMONGRASS BEEF WITH NOODLES

Bún bò xào

Although this is an easy dish to make, it carries a range of distinct but complementary flavours and textures. If you are using a small wok, cook the beef in batches so the wok stays very hot.

500 g beef scotch fillet

3 lemongrass stems, white part only, chopped

3 garlic cloves, chopped

1 tablespoon fish sauce

⅓ teaspoon freshly ground black pepper

600 g rice vermicelli

oil, for frying

1 cucumber, seeded and thinly sliced

90 g bean sprouts

½ small iceberg lettuce, sliced

1 teaspoon rice vinegar

1 tablespoon fish sauce, extra

1 handful Vietnamese mint sprigs

1 handful mint sprigs

90 g roasted unsalted peanuts, chopped

2 tablespoons fried shallots (see page 189)

vegetable pickle (see page 190) to serve

....
Serves 6
....

Thinly slice the beef and combine with the lemongrass, garlic, fish sauce and pepper. Set aside for 20 minutes to allow the flavours to develop.

Soak the rice vermicelli in boiling water for 4–5 minutes. Stir to separate the noodles, then drain and refresh under cold water. Use kitchen scissors to cut the vermicelli into easy-to-manage lengths. Divide the vermicelli among six bowls.

Heat a large wok and add a little oil. Add the beef to the hot oil and stir-fry for 1–2 minutes, until fragrant. Keep the ingredients moving so they do not stick or burn.

Add the cucumber, bean sprouts and lettuce and toss to combine. Add the rice vinegar, extra fish sauce, herbs and half the peanuts and toss to combine.

Immediately spoon the beef mixture onto the noodles. Sprinkle with the remaining peanuts and fried shallots and serve with the vegetable pickle.

BAGUETTES
–
SALADS

SALT STEAMED CHICKEN IN BAGUETTE

Banh mi kẹp gà hấp muối

To dry-steam the chicken you will need a heavy earthenware pot that can be placed directly over a gas burner. We like to cook a whole chicken and serve half on baguettes and the other half with steamed rice and bok choy.

1.6 kg chicken

1 kg coarse salt

2 banana leaves

4 lemongrass stems, white part only, crushed

3 handfuls Vietnamese mint leaves

4 cm knob of ginger, sliced

6 small baguettes

60 g mayonnaise

1 iceberg or other crisp green lettuce, leaves separated

1 cucumber, sliced

1 handful Vietnamese mint sprigs, extra

1 long red chilli, sliced

1½ tablespoons soy sauce

Serves 6

Remove the neck and giblets from the chicken and cut off any excess fat. Wash the chicken under cold running water, then pat dry.

Put the salt in an earthenware pot. Cut two pieces of banana leaf the size of the chicken, then place one on top of the salt. Lay the lemongrass in a row on top of the banana leaf and place the chicken on top so that it does not directly touch the salt. Put the Vietnamese mint on and around the chicken, then sprinkle over the ginger and cover with the remaining banana leaf.

Cover and cook the chicken over low heat for 45 minutes. Remove from the heat and set aside with the lid on for a further 15 minutes.

Cut the chicken in half. Take the meat off one half and reserve the other for a later use.

Preheat the oven to 180°C (Gas 4). Heat the baguettes in the oven for 1 minute, then cut in half lengthways and remove some of the soft centre.

Spread the mayonnaise on the bottom of the baguettes and top with the lettuce, cucumber, chicken, extra mint and chilli. Drizzle with the soy sauce and serve immediately.

GREEN PAPAYA SALAD

Nộm đu đu xanh

There is a tradition among itinerant street vendors of using a particular identifying sound to attract customers. Legend has it that in the days before cars and motorbikes, Hanoi was such a quiet city the most famous green papaya vendor in town could lure customers out of their houses with the sound of snipping metal scissors – his unique signal.

Nowadays, these subtle signals have often been replaced with a piece of recorded music blaring from a portable speaker to drown out the street noise.

1 green papaya

100 g bean sprouts

4 red Asian shallots, thinly sliced

½ handful coriander sprigs

3 tablespoons roasted peanuts, chopped

30 g dried beef

2 tablespoons fried shallots (see page 189)

Dressing

120 g sugar

100 ml lime juice

3 tablespoons fish sauce

1 long red chilli, seeded and thinly sliced

2 garlic cloves, chopped

....
Serves 6
....

Peel and thinly slice the green papaya into 4–6 cm long strips. Place the papaya in a bowl with the bean sprouts, Asian shallots, coriander, peanuts and dried beef.

For the dressing, combine the sugar and lime juice in a small bowl and stir until the sugar has dissolved. Add the fish sauce, chilli and garlic.

Pour the dressing over the salad and gently toss. Serve the salad in a large bowl, sprinkled with fried shallots.

BAGUETTE WITH PATE AND COLD CUTS

Bánh mì pa tê

We particularly like roast pork or char su, which can be purchased at Asian cafes, as fillings. Alternatively, ham or poached chicken are also good. Fried tofu can be added for some extra crunch.

6 small baguettes

120 g mayonnaise

180 g chicken liver pâté

12 slices of your favourite cooked meat

3 long red chillies, thinly sliced

60 g coriander sprigs

3 cucumbers, sliced

200 g carrot and daikon pickle (see page 190)

1½ tablespoons classic dipping sauce (see page 186)

Serves 6

Preheat the oven to 180°C (Gas 4). Heat the baguettes in the oven for 1 minute, then cut in half lengthways and remove some of the soft centre.

Spread the mayonnaise on the top half of each baguette and the pâté on the bottom half. Fill the centre with the cooked meat, chilli, coriander, cucumber and pickle.

Drizzle the dipping sauce over the baguette filling.

LEMONGRASS BEEF SKEWERS IN BAGUETTES

Bánh mì kẹp bò xiên sả

Vendors of this popular late afternoon snack vigorously fan
their braziers, not only to keep the charcoals burning but to
disperse the tantalising aroma of the grilled marinated meat
among the hungry after-work crowds.

300 g rump steak

2 red Asian shallots, roughly chopped

3 garlic cloves, roughly chopped

3 lemongrass stems, white part only,
roughly chopped

1 long red chilli, seeded and roughly
chopped

1 tablespoon toasted sesame seeds

2 teaspoons fish sauce

6 small baguettes

1 iceberg or other crisp green lettuce,
leaves separated

2 cucumbers, peeled and sliced

1 handful coriander sprigs

1 long red chilli, extra, sliced

....

Serves 6

....

Thinly slice the steak and place in a bowl. Place the
shallots, garlic, lemongrass and chilli in a large mortar
and use the pestle to grind the mixture into a fine paste.
Add the sesame seeds and crush with the pestle. Spoon
the paste and the fish sauce over the meat, cover and
refrigerate for I hour. Soak 12 bamboo skewers in water
for I hour to prevent them from burning during cooking.

Thread the meat onto the skewers and cook on a hot
chargrill or barbecue grill for 2–3 minutes on each side.

Meanwhile, split the baguettes in half lengthways. Place
the lettuce, cucumber, coriander sprigs and extra chilli
inside the baguettes.

Place two of the cooked skewers inside each baguette.
Hold onto the baguette and gently pull out the skewers.

EEL SALAD WITH CELLOPHANE NOODLES AND MINT

Miến lươn trộn

Eel is liked both for its taste and for its supposed health qualities. The Vietnamese distinguish between so-called 'hot' and 'cold' foods, which does not relate to temperature but to the idea of yin and yang. Eel is considered a 'cold' food, so to unfold its full health potential, it needs to be balanced with 'hot' ingredients – in this case, mint, pepper and chilli.

This dish does not only balance the yin and the yang, the wonderfully crunchy deep-fried eel and the chewy cellophane noodles also make a great contrast of textures.

3 small eels, skin and bones removed

⅓ teaspoon ground turmeric

large pinch of chilli powder

oil, for deep-frying

salt

200 g cellophane noodles

1 tablespoon sesame oil

½ handful Vietnamese mint leaves

8 spring onions, sliced

40 g roasted unsalted peanuts, chopped

40 g fried shallots (see page 189)

1 teaspoon fish sauce

⅓ teaspoon salt, extra

¼ teaspoon freshly ground black pepper

Serves 6

Cut the eel into 4 cm long pieces, then cut each piece lengthways into three. Rinse and pat dry with paper towel. Rub the ground turmeric and chilli powder into the eel pieces.

Heat the oil in a deep frying pan or wok and deep-fry the eel in batches until crisp. Drain well on paper towel and sprinkle with salt.

Meanwhile, soak the cellophane noodles in hot water for 10 minutes, then drain. Toss the sesame oil through the noodles and put them in a large bowl.

Add the Vietnamese mint, spring onion, half of the peanuts and half the shallots to the noodles. Drizzle the fish sauce over the noodles, sprinkle with the extra salt and pepper and toss to combine.

Transfer the noodles to a large platter and top with the eel and the remaining peanuts and shallots.

OMELETTE BAGUETTE

Bánh mì trứng

Simple but delicious! Wrapped in a sheet of newspaper, this is a popular breakfast for people on the run. Often, the Vietnamese will simply pull up with their motorcycle at their favourite *banh mi* cart to pick one up on the way to work.

12 eggs

½ teaspoon fish sauce

pinch of salt

⅓ teaspoon freshly ground black pepper

oil, for frying

6 small baguettes

2 cucumbers, peeled and sliced

1 handful coriander sprigs

1 long red chilli, sliced

1 tablespoon soy sauce

....
Serves 6
....

Break 2 eggs at a time into a small bowl, add some of the fish sauce, salt and pepper and lightly whisk to combine.

Heat some oil in a frying pan. Add the egg mixture and tilt the pan to cover the base. Use a wooden spoon or chopsticks to gently stir the egg, allowing the raw egg to run to the bottom. Leave for a further minute to finish the cooking process.

Split the baguettes in half lengthways. Place the omelette inside a baguette and top with some cucumber, coriander and chilli. Drizzle with a little soy sauce and serve hot. Repeat this process with the remaining egg mixture and baguettes.

LOTUS ROOT SALAD

Nộm ngó sen

The lotus flower is highly versatile and the entire lotus plant is used: the seeds in soups and desserts, the root in salads and stir-fries, the leaves for wrapping foods prior to cooking, and the flower for decoration and tea.

Although the ingredient in this recipe is commonly referred to as the root, it is in fact the tendril that runs off the large rhizome-shaped root.

1 chicken breast fillet

250 g pickled lotus root

100 g bean sprouts

1 carrot, cut into thin strips

3 red Asian shallots, thinly sliced

3 tablespoons Vietnamese mint sprigs

1 tablespoon mint sprigs

2 tablespoons toasted sesame seeds, plus 2 teaspoons to serve

2 tablespoons fried shallots (see page 189), plus 1 teaspoon to serve

1 long red chilli, seeded and cut into thin strips

Dressing

120 g sugar

100 ml lime juice

3 tablespoons fish sauce

2 garlic cloves, chopped

....
Serves 6
....

Bring a small saucepan of salted water to the boil. Add the chicken breast, reduce the heat and simmer for 8–10 minutes. Transfer the chicken to a board. Cool, then cut the chicken into thin slices.

Rinse the lotus root to remove some of the pickling liquid. Drain well and pat dry. Cut the lotus root lengthways into four pieces.

To make the dressing, whisk together the sugar and lime juice until the sugar has completely dissolved. Add the fish sauce and garlic.

Put the lotus root, chicken, bean sprouts, carrot, shallots, herbs, sesame seeds, fried shallots and chilli in a bowl, pour on the dressing and gently toss to combine.

Serve the salad on a large platter, sprinkled with the extra sesame seeds and fried shallots.

FISH PATTIES WITH CORIANDER AND CHILLI IN BAGUETTE

Bánh mì chả cá

On the southern Con Dao islands and on Phu Quoc this is a favourite sandwich filling. You could also coat the fish patties in green rice for some extra crunch, then fry them and serve with the classic dipping sauce (see page 186).

600 g snapper fillets

2 garlic cloves, chopped

1 tablespoon fish sauce

½ teaspoon sugar

⅓ teaspoon salt

½ teaspoon freshly ground black pepper

3 spring onions, white part only, thinly sliced

oil, for deep-frying

6 small baguettes

3 tablespoons mayonnaise

1 iceberg or other crisp green lettuce, leaves separated

1 cucumber, sliced

120 g tofu, cut into 2 cm thick slices (optional)

1 handful coriander sprigs

1 long red chilli, sliced

1½ tablespoons soy sauce

....
Serves 6
....

Remove the skin and bones from the snapper fillets and cut the fish into rough chunks. Put the fish and garlic in a food processor and process to a paste. Add the fish sauce, sugar, salt, pepper and spring onion and process until combined. Cover and refrigerate for 30 minutes.

Using lightly oiled fingers, form the fish mixture into 12 patties.

Heat the oil in a deep frying pan or wok and deep-fry the patties for 4–5 minutes, or until they are golden and cooked through. Drain well on paper towel.

Preheat the oven to 180°C (Gas 4). Heat the baguettes in the oven for 1 minute, then cut in half lengthways and remove some of the soft centre.

Spread the mayonnaise on the bottom of the baguettes and top with the lettuce, cucumber, tofu (if using), fish patties, coriander and chilli. Drizzle with the soy sauce and serve immediately.

SWEETS

GINGER STICKY RICE CAKES

Chè con ong

This is a very popular dessert during the lunar New Year holiday period. Wooden moulds are used to make many sticky rice dishes. The moulds have a removable base that is carved with a decorative pattern on the inside. Asian grocery stores and specialty kitchenware stores stock a variety of these moulds.

400 g glutinous rice

pinch of salt

4 cm knob of ginger, roughly chopped

100 g palm sugar, ground or grated to a fine powder

1 tablespoon toasted sesame seeds

Serves 6

Put the rice in a bowl, cover with cold water and leave to soak for 2 hours.

Drain the rice and place in a saucepan. Add enough cold water to just cover the rice. Add the salt and bring to the boil over medium heat. Stir the rice, cover and reduce the heat to low. Cook for 10 minutes, or until the rice is tender. Remove from the heat.

Meanwhile, using a mortar and pestle, pound the ginger to extract the juice. Squeeze the crushed ginger pieces with your hand to extract the remaining juice. Discard the ginger pieces.

Use a pair of chopsticks to stir the palm sugar and ginger juice through the rice, being careful not to break the rice grains. Cover and set aside for 5 minutes, or until all the liquid has been absorbed.

Fold half of the toasted sesame seeds through the rice. Line two wooden moulds or bowls with plastic wrap and sprinkle in the remaining sesame seeds. Lightly press the rice into the moulds and set aside to cool.

Carefully turn the rice out of the moulds onto small plates. Serve with Vietnamese green tea.

FRUIT CUP

Hoa quả dầm

The fondness of the Vietnamese for sweetened condensed milk is
another culinary legacy of colonial rule. Dairy giant Royal Friesland Foods,
one of Vietnam's biggest milk producers, for example, is able to trace
back its involvement with the region to 1924, when they first imported
150 cartons of canned, sweetened milk for the homesick French in Hanoi.

1 kg mixed seasonal fruits, diced

1 tablespoon mint, chopped

2 cups crushed ice

600 g thick plain yoghurt

80 ml coconut milk

1½ tablespoons sweetened
condensed milk

6 mint sprigs

....

Serves 6

....

Put the diced fruit and chopped mint in a large bowl
and toss gently to combine. Put the crushed ice in the
bottom of six tall glasses, then spoon in the fruit.

Combine the yoghurt, coconut milk and condensed milk
in a jug, then pour over the fruit. Serve garnished with
the mint sprigs.

BANH TROI STALL
Phạm Bằng

Phạm Bang is as close as one gets to Hanoi royalty. The eighty-year-old actor is the fourth generation of his family to be born in the historic old quarter, and for the last sixty years he has lived in the same building in Hang Giay Street. Well-loved by the locals for his comedy skits, which air every weekend on both national and local television stations, the sprightly octogenarian is also famous for selling sweet dumplings. Almost every afternoon he sets up shop in front of the wooden gate leading to his upstairs room in the back building of a typical old-quarter house.

Born into a solid middle-class family with both parents working as school teachers, Bang grew up in colonial times and speaks fluent French. He caught the acting bug early in life and recalls how unhappy his parents were with his choice of career. Their worries seemed to bear out when, after twenty years in the acting business, his career couldn't support him and his family.

In the late 1970s, Bang urgently needed an additional source of income and he turned to dumpling making. For a short time he worked with a Chinese business partner, but as the Chinese left the area, he struck out on his own. 'Basically I am self-taught and it took me four years to perfect my recipe for *banh troi*,' Bang says proudly. The effort paid off and his stall is well known beyond the local area, and not just because of its famous proprietor.

'The secret to a good *banh troi* lies in the consistency of the dough,' says Bang, who adds a small amount of regular rice flour to the glutinous rice flour. He uses 20 to 30 kilograms of flour a day, and starts making his dough just after sunrise. By midmorning most of the available surfaces in the large room Bang occupies are covered with trays of raw dumplings, ready for the steamer. Bang makes two types of dumpling: one filled with grated coconut, the other with black sesame seeds. Customers get one of each type per serve unless otherwise requested.

While acting alone couldn't pay the bills in the 1980s and early 1990s, Bang's fame as an actor not only promoted the stall, but also helped him keep it going through the difficult *bao cap* time of food rationing. Vietnam's economy, along with Bang's professional situation, improved over the next two decades. Bang could have retired from dumpling making a long time ago, but the small section of footpath remains his personal stage. 'I also do it,' he says, 'out of respect for the trade that allowed me to carry on as a performer.'

It looks like the twin traditions of cooking and acting are set to continue. Out of his four children, only one has chosen a career in the world of business. Two of his daughters have become actresses, and the third is helping Bang keep the stall going.

BANANA AND COCONUT SOUP

Chè chuối

Although main meals mostly conclude with a simple plate of cut fruit, the Vietnamese have a very sweet tooth and snack on sugary treats throughout the day. During winter, these treats tend to be hot sweet soups in the north of the country, while in summer or in the tropical south, *che* is served over ice in tall glasses.

6 bananas

400 ml coconut milk

3 tablespoons sugar

2 tablespoons toasted sesame seeds

2 tablespoons roasted unsalted peanuts

....
Serves 6
....

Peel the bananas and cut them in half lengthways. Cook under a hot grill until golden.

Meanwhile, combine the coconut milk and sugar in a saucepan and gently cook over low heat until the sugar has dissolved.

Add the grilled banana and simmer until the banana has softened. Spoon the soup into six bowls and serve sprinkled with the sesame seeds and peanuts.

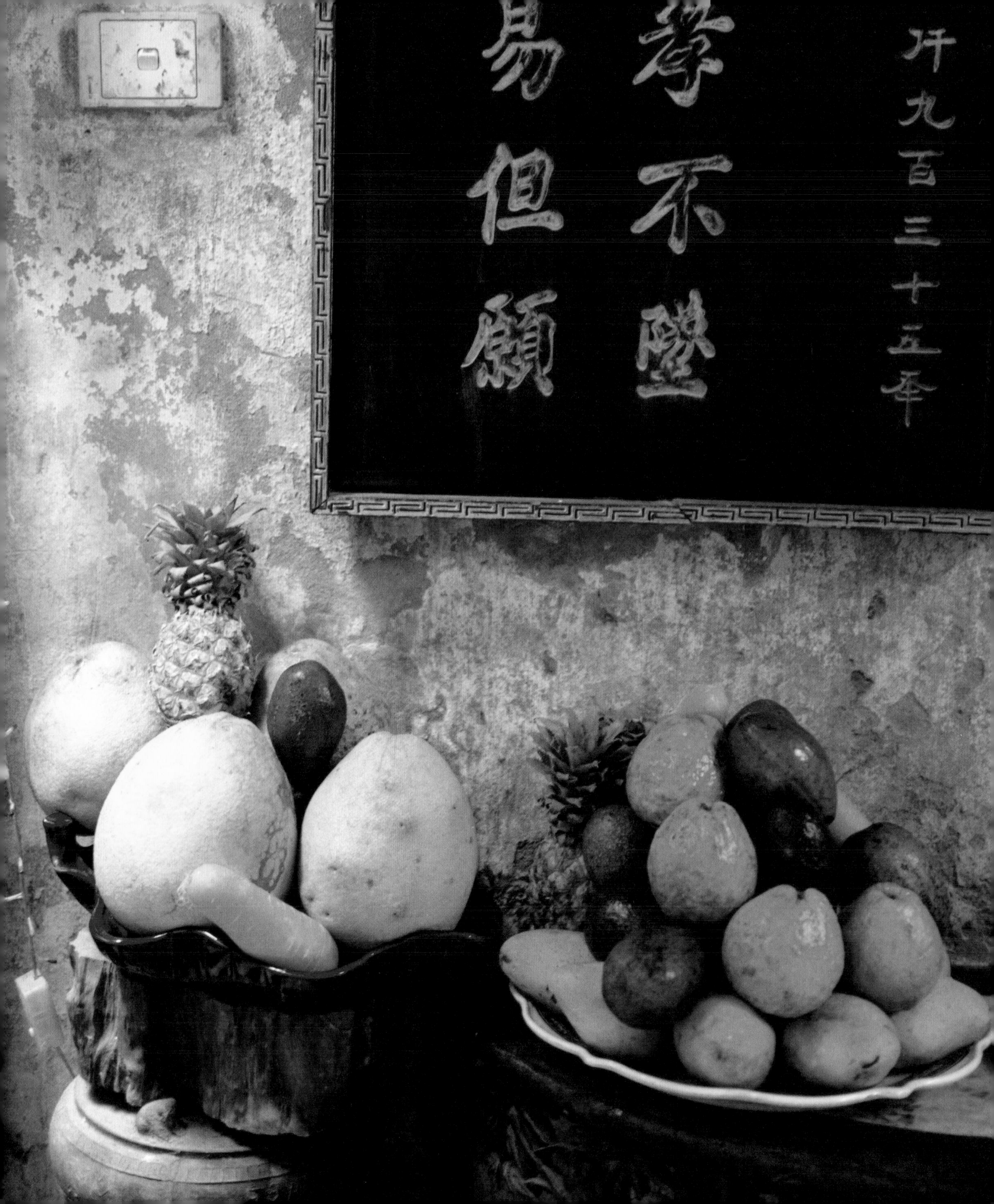
仟九百三十五年
孝不墜
易但願

BLACK SESAME SEED AND PEANUT SOUP

Chè mè đen

This shiny black sweet soup is one of the few foods
of this colour in world cuisine.

If pandan leaves are unavailable, pandan essence can
be used as a substitute. You will find it in specialty
shops or the pastry sections of good supermarkets.

250 g toasted black sesame seeds

200 g roasted unsalted peanuts

200 g raw sugar

400 ml coconut milk

2 pandan leaves

....

Serves 6

....

Put the sesame seeds and peanuts in a food processor,
and chop until they are finely ground.

Meanwhile, put the raw sugar and 250 ml of water in
a saucepan over low heat. Gently bring the syrup to the
boil, stirring occasionally. Add the ground sesame seeds
and peanuts, along with 350 ml of the coconut milk and
the pandan leaves. Cook the soup, stirring occasionally,
for 5 minutes, or until it thickens. Remove and discard
the pandan leaves.

Spoon the soup into six small bowls and garnish with
the remaining coconut milk.

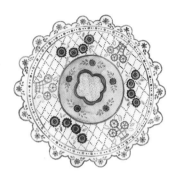
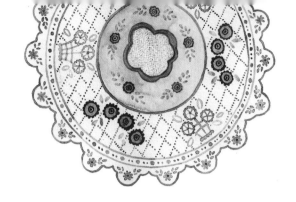

SILKEN TOFU IN GINGER SYRUP

Tào phớ

Sweetened tofu is usually offered by roaming vendors
selling from metal drums attached like panniers
to the pack-racks of their bicycles. In a clever sales
strategy, they will often position themselves near
schools to tempt hungry children on their way home.

Older ginger will overpower this dish, so make sure
you use younger, sweeter roots.

300 g sugar

4 cm knob of young ginger, thinly sliced

juice of 1 mandarin

500 g silken tofu

6 jasmine flowers

....
Serves 6
....

Put the sugar and 500 ml of water in a saucepan. Slowly
bring to the boil, stirring until the sugar has completely
dissolved. Add the ginger slices and mandarin juice, then
simmer for 5 minutes.

Meanwhile, cut the tofu into 5 mm thick slices. Remove
the saucepan from the heat and gently lower the tofu
into the ginger syrup. Add the jasmine flowers and leave
for at least 15 minutes before serving to allow the tofu to
absorb the flavours from the syrup.

Serve the tofu and syrup in six small bowls.

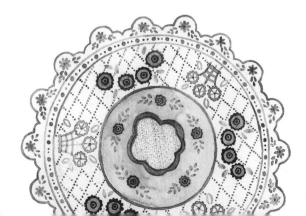

MUNG BEAN CAKES

Chè kho

On every first day of the lunar month, market vendors produce these little cakes for sale at their stalls. They are a popular offering at altars for the ancestors and can, of course, be enjoyed by the living after the joss sticks have burnt down.

500 g dried mung beans

½ cup sugar

2 tablespoons grated coconut

½ teaspoon salt

....

Serves 6

....

Put the mung beans in a large bowl, cover with cold water and leave to soak for 3 hours. Drain well and put the mung beans in a small saucepan with enough cold water to cover them. Cook the mung beans over low heat for 30–40 minutes, or until they are soft.

Drain the mung beans. Use a food processor or mortar and pestle to process or pound the mung beans into a smooth paste.

Combine the sugar and 125 ml of water in a small saucepan. Cook over low heat, stirring until the sugar has dissolved. Add the mung bean paste, coconut and salt, and cook until the mixture is thick and creamy.

Line two wooden moulds or bowls with plastic wrap. Spoon the mung bean mixture into the moulds and press it down, then set aside to cool.

Turn the mung bean cakes out of the moulds and onto small plates. Serve with Vietnamese green tea.

SAUCES
–
CONDIMENTS

CLASSIC DIPPING SAUCE

Nước chấm truyền thống

3 tablespoons fish sauce

100 ml lime juice

1 teaspoon rice vinegar

½ cup sugar

2 garlic cloves, finely chopped

1 long red chilli, finely chopped

....
Serves 6
....

Combine the fish sauce, lime juice, rice vinegar and sugar in a small bowl. Stir until the sugar has completely dissolved.

Add the garlic and chilli and serve in dipping bowls.

SOY CHILLI DIPPING SAUCE

Xi dầu ớt

120 ml soy sauce

juice of ½ lime

¼ teaspoon sugar

½ long red chilli, cut into thin rings

....
Serves 6
....

Combine the soy sauce, lime juice and sugar in a small bowl. Stir until the sugar has completely dissolved.

Divide the sauce among six dipping bowls and add the chilli.

HOISIN DIPPING SAUCE
Nước chấm hoi sin

70 g roasted unsalted peanuts, chopped
oil, for frying
2 garlic cloves, chopped
100 ml hoisin sauce
1 red birdseye chilli, seeded and chopped

....
Serves 6
....

Put half the peanuts in a mortar and grind them to a coarse powder.

Heat a little oil in a small saucepan. Cook the garlic until fragrant, add the ground peanuts and toss. Add the hoisin sauce, 1½ tablespoons of water (or use the liquid reserved from soaking dried shrimp to enhance the flavour) and half the chilli and cook for a further 2 minutes. If the sauce is too thick, add a little more water until it reaches the correct consistency.

Remove the sauce from the heat and divide it among six dipping bowls. When the sauce is cool, scatter the remaining peanuts and chilli on top.

GINGER DIPPING SAUCE
Nước mắm gừng

120 ml fish sauce
1 teaspoon sugar
2 cm knob of ginger, thinly sliced
3 garlic cloves, chopped
1 long red chilli, chopped

....
Serves 6
....

Combine the fish sauce and sugar in a small bowl. Stir until the sugar has completely dissolved.

Add the ginger, garlic and chilli and serve in six dipping bowls.

BUN CHA DIPPING SAUCE
Nước chấm bún chả

300 g sugar

100 ml fish sauce

100 ml rice vinegar

100 ml lime juice

1 long red chilli, seeded and chopped

3 garlic cloves, chopped

60 g carrot, cut into 3 cm pieces

60 g green papaya, cut into 3 cm pieces

Serves 6

Combine the sugar, fish sauce and rice vinegar in a small saucepan. Stir over low heat until the sugar has completely dissolved. Allow to cool.

Add 200 ml of water and the remaining ingredients and serve in dipping bowls.

VEGAN DIPPING SAUCE
Nước chấm chay

2 tablespoons soy sauce

1 tablespoon rice vinegar

1 tablespoon lemon juice

pinch of sugar

pinch of salt

½ long red chilli, seeded and finely chopped

2 garlic cloves, finely chopped

50 g green papaya, cut into 2 cm pieces

Serves 6

Put the soy sauce, rice vinegar, lemon juice, sugar, salt and 3 tablespoons of water in a small bowl and whisk to combine.

Add the chilli, garlic and papaya and serve in six dipping bowls.

LIME, SALT AND CHILLI

Muối chanh ớt

½ teaspoon sea salt

2–3 thin birdseye chilli rings or cracked
  black pepper

¼ small lime

....
Serves 1
....

Mould the salt into a mound in a dipping bowl. Put
the chilli or pepper next to the salt, and put the lime
wedge beside the chilli or pepper.

When the rest of the food is presented at the table,
squeeze the lime juice into the dipping bowl and stir
with a chopstick to incorporate the flavours.

FRIED SHALLOTS

Hành phi

8 red Asian shallots

vegetable or peanut oil, for
  deep-frying

....
Makes about 2 tablespoons (40 g)
....

Peel and thinly slice the shallots lengthways. They
should all be the same thickness so that they will
cook evenly.

Pour the oil into a wok or saucepan, allowing room
for the oil to rise when the shallots are added. Heat
the oil until it is hot but not smoking. The oil is ready
when a piece of shallot sizzles when it hits the oil.
Add half the shallots and cook until they are golden
brown, carefully stirring them with a metal spoon
to ensure even cooking. Remove the shallots with a
slotted spoon and drain on paper towel. Repeat with
the remaining shallots.

Store the cooled shallots in a sealed jar. Fried shallots
are best eaten on the day they are cooked.

VEGETABLE PICKLE
Dưa mûoi

1 carrot, thinly sliced

200 g green papaya, peeled and thinly sliced

½ teaspoon salt

3 tablespoons sugar

3 tablespoons rice vinegar

2 tablespoons fish sauce

1 long red chilli, seeded and finely chopped

2 garlic cloves, finely chopped

Serves 6

Put the carrot and papaya in a bowl and sprinkle with the salt. Allow to sit for 5 minutes, then rinse off the salt and pat dry with paper towel.

Combine the carrot and papaya with the sugar, rice vinegar, fish sauce, chilli and garlic.

Store the pickle in a sealed jar in the refrigerator for up to two days.

CARROT AND DAIKON PICKLE
Dưa góp

250 g carrots

200 g daikon

200 ml rice vinegar

½ cup sugar

2 teaspoons salt

Makes about 2 cups

Peel the carrots and daikon, cut into 5 cm batons and place in a jar with a lid.

To make the pickling liquid, combine the vinegar, sugar, salt and 250 ml of water in a small saucepan. Heat until the sugar has completely dissolved, then cool until lukewarm.

Pour the pickling liquid over the vegetables and leave for at least 1 hour before serving.

Store in the refrigerator for up to 2 weeks.

ANNATTO OIL
Dầu điều

500 ml canola oil

2 tablespoons annatto seeds

....

Makes 500 ml

....

Put the canola oil and annatto seeds in a saucepan and gently heat for 1 hour, or until the oil takes on a deep red colour. Do not allow the oil to boil or become too hot or it will taste bitter.

When the oil is completely cool, strain it through a fine sieve and discard the annatto seeds.

Store the oil in a sealed jar for up to 4 weeks.

TAMARIND WATER
sốt me

200 g tamarind pulp

....

Makes 500 ml

....

Break the tamarind pulp into small pieces and put in a bowl. Add 100 ml of warm water and soak for 15 minutes. While the pulp is soaking, mash it with a spoon.

Pass the mixture through a sieve and discard the tamarind seeds.

Store the tamarind water in the refrigerator for 2–3 weeks.

GLOSSARY

NOODLES

No Vietnamese meal would be complete without rice, but steamed rice can be difficult to prepare on the streets. Luckily rice can be served in many ways. Ground into flour. Vietnam's most versatile staple is the basis for rice paper wrappers, dumpling dough and noodles.

In many ways, noodles are the ideal street food: they can be eaten fresh, cooked in broths, steamed or fried, while being easily transportable. The making of fresh noodles is still very much a cottage industry in Vietnam and visitors can find entire villages throughout the country that specialise in the craft of noodle making.

Bun (Rice Vermicelli)

Dough made from glutinous rice and water is pressed through a perforated container into boiling water to form thin, round noodles. After a few seconds in the boiling water, the noodles are removed and chilled. With *bun*, fresh is best. These chewy noodles have a shelf life of only 4 hours before losing their texture.

Bun is a culinary 'all rounder' – often served as a cold side dish with a dipping sauce like in the famous *bun cha*, but it can also be added to broths or fresh spring rolls.

Banh Hoi

Banh hoi are made from a similar dough to bun. They are very fine noodles and the delicate strands are interwoven into small squares. *Banh hoi* are served cold, often topped with roasted or grilled meats and accompanied by a dipping sauce.

Pho

Pho noodles are made from steamed noodle sheets, and the quality of the sheets is judged by their unblemished silky surface. The sheets can be used as a wrap for *pho cuon* (beef rice paper rolls), for example, or they can be cut into noodles: fettuccine-width for stir-fries and slightly narrower for the famous noodle soup of the same name.

Mi Quang

Mi are Chinese-style egg noodles and *mi quang* originated in the centre of Vietnam around the city of Danang and in Quang Nam Province, where noodle-makers often add turmeric to the dough as extra seasoning. The soft noodle has a similar texture to Japanese udon noodles and is used together with wontons, another ingredient Vietnam inherited from China.

Banh Da Haiphong

A variety from the northern port city of Haiphong, this reddish-brown noodle is firmer than *bun* or *pho*, which makes it ideal for *lau* (hotpot), where it is cooked at the very end of the meal in the rich broth.

Mien (Cellophane Noodles)

Not made from rice but from starch, these translucent, skinny noodles are the odd one out. The most popular variety, *mien*, are produced from mung beans, others from cassava or canna. Also known as glass noodles, they are sold in dried bundles and need to be soaked in boiling water before they can be used to add texture to fried spring rolls and salads.

Dried *Bun*

Fresh *Bun*

Banh Hoi

Fresh *Pho*

Dried *Pho*

Pho Sheets

Mi Quang

Banh Da Haiphong

Mien

HERBS

Any visit to a local market will reveal the three foundation stones of Vietnamese cuisine: rice, fish sauce and, very importantly, herbs. In fact, Vietnam's cooking is renowned for its judicious and subtle use of aromatics, which are offered in abundance and bought by the bagful. In a cuisine that is often described as fragrant, herbs are often used raw or added at the very end of the cooking process, as their subtle perfume would otherwise disappear. They are prized for both their flavours and their health properties, being an important source of minerals and vitamins.

This glossary covers the herbs used in the recipes and is by no means meant to be an exhaustive list of the wide range of herbs used in Vietnamese cooking.

Thai Basil

A much-loved herb in both Mediterranean and Asian cuisines, basil boasts more than 12 varieties. The flavours of the varieties grouped together under the name of Thai basil are very different from the sweet aromas characterising their European counterparts.

There are three main types used in Vietnamese cooking: Thai sweet basil possesses a mild flavour with hints of anise. Prone to losing much of its aroma during cooking, it is often used as a garnish. Holy basil, on the other hand, has a more robust, peppery flavour that unfolds during the cooking process and is a favourite for stir-fries. Finally there is Thai lemon basil, also sold under the name of hoary basil, the lime aroma of which goes particularly well with seafood.

Betel Leaf

This heart-shaped leaf belongs to a vine that attaches itself to the areca nut tree (which, by power of association, is often erroneously called the betel nut tree). Belonging to the *piperaceae* family, which also includes the pepper plant, the leaf can be quite tough and is rarely eaten raw. Used mainly in stews or as a wrap for chargrilling, it infuses a subtly bitter taste and is said to have antiseptic properties.

Vietnamese Mint

Not part of the mint family, but rather a smart weed or pink weed, the taste of the pointy leaves with their purple tips is similar to coriander with a strong lemony note. It is said to also possess digestive qualities. In the north, Vietnamese mint is often paired with duck and other dark meats, and the best Vietnamese mint is said to come from Lang village near Hanoi.

Saw Tooth Herb

Named because of its long leaves with their serrated edges, this herb is native to the Caribbean Islands but has become very common in South-East Asia. It is also known as saw tooth coriander and is similar in taste to regular coriander, only with a stronger aroma, and is used as a garnish or in soups and stir-fries. Because the leaves are larger, they can also be used as wraps.

Thai Basil

Betel Leaf

Vietnamese Mint

Saw Tooth Herb

Dill

Mint

Dill

A native to southern Russia and western Africa, this herb made its way via the Mediterranean to Vietnam. Dill is also known as Laotian coriander, although it belongs to the family of herbs that includes parsley, cumin and bay leaf. The sweet, yet tangy flavour of the fern-like leaves goes particularly well with seafood. Dill needs to be very fresh to unfold its full aroma and should be added only at the very end of the cooking process.

Mint

Indigenous to the Mediterranean, mint has been known since antiquity. Legend has it that it was named after a nymph called Minthe. In a fit of jealousy, Pluto's wife turned her into a plant, and while Pluto was powerless to reverse the spell, he at least could impart the plant with its distinct perfume. There are up to twenty different kinds of mint, with spearmint being the most common variety for cooking, adding a fresh, cool taste to savoury dishes. The herb is also an excellent source of vitamins A and C.

Pandan Leaf

Pandan Leaf

This long and pointy leaf is harvested from the pandanus palm, also known as screw pine. The leaves are not actually eaten but are added during the cooking process to impart a complex flavour, often described as grassy and sweet with hints of hazelnut. Featuring mainly in south Vietnamese dishes and often paired up with coconut, the liquid from the leaves is also used as a natural food colouring for cakes. The pandan extract that is commercially available is often enhanced with green food colouring.

Spring Onion

Spring Onion

Rich in vitamin C, this slim and bulbless variety of scallion is used both raw and cooked. Also known as 'bunching onions' because they are sold in bundles held together by a string or rubber band, spring onions add a fresh, mild onion taste and a vibrant green colour to cooked dishes and salads.

Lemongrass

Lemongrass

Like coriander, lemongrass is an essential ingredient in Vietnamese cuisine. Botanically speaking a tufted grass, the herb contains the same essential oil that is present in lemon rind, giving lemongrass its unique citrus aroma with just a hint of ginger. For most recipes the tough, fibrous outer layers are removed to reveal the white bulb of the plant, which is then either chopped or bruised with a mortar and pestle.

Perilla

Perilla

A distant cousin of the mint family, this vine leaf with serrated edges is also sold under the names of Chinese basil or wild sesame. Indigenous to South-East and East Asia, the Vietnamese variety of the perilla leaf is green on one side and purple on the other. A good source of minerals and vitamins, this fragrant herb is eaten as garnish with *bun* (vermicelli) dishes, as well as in soups and stews.

Lotus Leaf

Although the lotus plant grows in muddy ponds and puddles, it has become a symbol for purity.
Part of the reason might be the 'lotus effect', referring to the self-cleansing properties of the leaves thanks to their complex molecular structure and waxy surface. Given that the large, fan-shaped leaves are naturally clean, it is only logical that they are used as food wrappers, imparting their subtle earthy aroma into sticky rice and other dishes.

Lotus Leaf

Kaffir Lime Leaf

A South-East Asian native, lime leaves are a popular ingredient in Thai, Cambodian and Vietnamese cuisines, imbuing a distinctly spicy citrus aroma to stews and curries.

Kaffir Lime Leaf

Coriander

This herb is sometimes referred to as Chinese parsley because of its similarity in appearance to the European flat-leaf parsley. While the dried seeds can also be used, it is the fresh leaves, also known as cilantro, that make it one of the most popular herbs in Vietnamese cooking.

Coriander is often eaten as a garnish, in salads or *banh mi* (baguettes). The aroma of coriander is fleeting so if it is used in hot dishes it needs to be added at the very end of the cooking process. To the European palate, the flavour is slightly soapy and can be an acquired taste. Coriander is also considered a good source of vitamins A, B and C.

Coriander

INDEX

ACKNOWLEDGEMENTS

Many friends have supported and encouraged us putting
this book together. We particularly wish to thank:

In Vietnam, the chefs at the Hanoi Cooking Centre for
sharing their knowledge and passion for Vietnamese food:
Nguyen Manh Hung, Nguyen Huu Y, Phan Thi Duyen
and Hoang Viet Linh.

Giang Van Quyet, Nguyen Viet Hung and Nguyen Thi Nga,
Do Tuan Anh, Cao Thi Than Thuy, Nguyen Thi Nhan Hoa
and our business partner Dinh Phung Linh for interpreting
and invaluable cultural insight.

Cynthia Mann, Rebecca Hales and Maria Poulos for reading
through earlier drafts and making them better.

We again very much enjoyed working with the team at
Hardie Grant Publishing in Australia and thank
Paul McNally for commissioning the book in the first place,
Jane Winning for seeing the project through and getting
it to print in a very short time, Justine Harding for her
judicious editing and Daniella Germain for turning words
and pictures into an eye-catching whole.

Published in 2011 by Hardie Grant Books

Hardie Grant Books (Australia)
Ground Floor, Building 1, 658 Church Street
Richmond, Victoria 3121
www.hardiegrant.com.au

Hardie Grant Books (UK)
Second Floor, North Suite
Dudley House
Southampton Street
London WC2E 7HF
www.hardiegrant.co.uk

Cataloguing-in-Publication data is available from the National Library of Australia.

ISBN 978 1 74270 142 4

Publisher: Paul McNally
Project editor: Jane Winning
Design and layout: Daniella Germain
Photography: Michael Fountoulakis
Copy editor: Justine Harding
Colour reproduction by Splitting Image Colour Studio
Printed in China by 1010 Printing International Limited